THE EXTRAORDINARY WITHIN

BY DONN SMITH
AND LYNN SUMIDA

National Library of Canada Cataloguing in Publication

Smith, Donn, 1951-
    The extraordinary within : welcoming change and unlocking our true essence / Donn Smith,
Lynn Sumida; editor, Sheila C. Jones.

Includes bibliographical references.
ISBN 0-9697585-4-5

    1. Change (Psychology) 2. Self-actualization (Psychology). 3. Smith, Donn, 1951-
I. Sumida, Lynn, 1951- II. Jones, Sheila C., 1937- III. Title.
BF637.C4S62 2003   158.1   C2003-906895-1

Produced by THE ART DEPARTMENT
a division of Canada Wide Magazines & Communications Ltd.

Project Director SANDY CRAWFORD
Editor SHEILA C. JONES
Production Supervisor GAIL TAKAHASHI
Project Manager CASEY CRAWFORD
Portrait Photography RON SANGHA

Printed in Canada by FRIESENS

TABLE OF CONTENTS

ACKNOWLEDGEMENTS

To Lynn Sumida, who, from the very beginning, had the vision of what this book could be. She spent hours and hours listening to me as I talked through one concept after another and then creatively found the words to express what I really wanted to say. At times, when the work seemed overwhelming, Lynn continued to move ahead with dogged determination. In short this book would never have been written without her.

I would like to acknowledge all that I learned in my life from my Mom and Dad, knowing that they did the best they could with the resources they had.

A special acknowledgement goes out to all my brothers and sisters: Rita, Ivan, Phyllis, Janet, Carol, David, Brenda, Arlene and Jamie. I recognize that every person perceives his or her family from a unique point of view and that I am telling my story from my own perspective. Others will have had a very different experience.

I would like to thank Wilma for being part of my journey over 30 years of marriage. The learning curve at times was very sharp. Thanks to my daughter Shelly who was a great mirror for me when I was holding onto something constricting, and for the wonderful laughter when I let go. To my son Trevor who kept challenging me with every word I spoke, in his determination to be himself. And to my beautiful grandchildren, Daniel and Makenzie for being strong beams of light.

To Sister Bethany Doyle who kept telling me to write a book and to every client who worked with me and trusted me. I learned an immense amount from each of you, no matter what the results were. I also appreciate all the professional teachers who added to my knowledge and challenged me along the way.

To Sherry Shaw-Froggett, who was so excited about me writing a book and who contributed tremendously by interviewing all the individuals whose stories appear in this book.

To Steve Davis who, in his always gentle way, made suggestion after suggestion on the proper meaning of concepts and ideas using his gift with the English language, and who also contributed research on many ideas used in this book.

Special thanks to Keith Kosick for working tirelessly on behalf of Excelanation, and specifically on this book. Your dedication to excellence and desire for this book to be the very best it could be, made a tremendous difference.

Lastly, to Rosy Lecky, my partner in all ways, who was a never-ending emotional support, living thesaurus and editor – thank you.

FOR TIME BEYOND MEMORY, SIAMESE MONKS HAD IN THEIR possession a large statue of the Buddha, made of clay. In 1957 when they began a renovation of the temple, the Buddha statue had to be relocated. They brought in a large crane, but the crane could not lift it. It was raining very hard that day so the monks covered the statue with a tarp. In the middle of the night, the monk in charge went out to make his routine check. He lifted the tarp and shone a flashlight on the statue. To his surprise he saw a glimmer showing through a crack in the clay. He got a chisel and a hammer and started to chip away at the clay that had been softened by the rain; it was eight inches thick. As it turned out, the giant Buddha, which was 10 feet, six inches tall, was covered with two tons of clay. The statue hidden under the clay was made of pure gold. The Golden Buddha is valued at $196 million.

Several hundred years earlier the Burmese Army had invaded Thailand. To protect their Golden Buddha from being stolen or melted down, the Siamese monks covered the statue with this thick coating of clay. But the monks were slain in the invasion and no one survived to tell how they had protected the Buddha.

We are like the Golden Buddha. All the experiences of the past (the clay) have covered us up and we cannot see our true essence. The stories you are about to read, including mine, describe the excavation of our human spirit, our true essence. The story begins with the clay, what creates it, how we label it and how we remove it. These stories are also about how people feel after the clay is removed. The exhilaration comes with washing away the pain and misconceptions about ourselves. After human beings remove the clay what is revealed is the extraordinary *within*.

INTRODUCTION

Somewhere, something incredible is waiting to be known.
Carl Sagan, 1934 – 1996

WITHIN EACH OF US ARE THE ORDINARY AND THE EXTRA-
ordinary. Within each of us is a core I call *True Essence*, which, if allowed,
can shine forth with immense power. But this is not how most of us think
of ourselves. Most of us walk around unaware of our true essence, living in
chaos and confusion as best we can. How do I know this essence exists?
Why do I think we are disconnected from it? If these questions sound like
the old, familiar questions about the meaning of life, they are. The only
difference is I know these questions can be answered. What's even more
surprising is that a boy, raised in a big, poor family riddled with addictions
and chaos, eventually found these answers.

As a child I knew a lot about the laws of survival, like the slowest eater
doesn't get fed, or survival of the fittest, which I thought meant if you have
to fight, hit the other guy first and hard. I was a little more confused about the
laws of love. They didn't seem to make much sense in our family. Oh, I saw

lots of love, but then I saw the opposite, all in the same person. Love often seemed to be just out of my reach. I tried pleasing people but I never got it quite right. And speaking of getting it right, religion confused me the most. It seemed everything was backwards. Instead of feeling great in church, I always felt afraid. I was caught in a swirling current of beliefs, pulling me down and telling me how bad and sinful I was and what I had done wrong.

What I did learn is that nature will allow each of us to go about as far as we can down the wrong path before we get the big wakeup call. I sure wish there had been an early warning sign that I was way off track. Or maybe there was an early warning and I didn't know how to read the signals.

Today, I have a whole new perspective on what humans are really all about and how the world can be a place of joy and peace and harmony. Most of which is the total opposite of what I learned as I grew up. I was taught to think small and not get too big for my britches. Today I know that the *genius* lives in each and every one of us. We aren't meant to think small, we are meant to think big and expansively, to live the dream within us. Our job is to discover how to do that and then act on our beliefs and passions.

Many of my thoughts and ideas seem to come from my curiosity. How curious are you? I have been curious my whole life – my parents and teachers can vouch for this. It wasn't always seen as positive. Thanks to this curiosity I have gone from the pits of despair to the heights of ecstasy – not drug-induced ecstasy, but the true one – and on the way discovered some amazing things. I discovered how people can transform health problems, how CEOs can balance their home and work life and be even more productive, and how athletes can perform with *effortless effort*. I've seen people literally change their personality, to be kind and generous, when before they were ruthless and deceitful. The key to all these changes lies within us, in a power that most of us have left untapped, in our *True Essence*. I discovered laws of nature I never knew about, and once I did, I connected with a power that was way beyond anything I had ever imagined.

I don't consider myself special, in the sense that I am the only one who can do this or that. In fact, I believe the very opposite. We are all extraordinary; we just don't know it. The examples I want to share with you are meant to shine a light in a dark corner and say: "See, this is possible." When I was in school, after failing three grades, I knew a lot about feeling hopeless and I certainly didn't feel special. What is remarkable is how little it took for me to try again, for hope to surge through my veins. One teacher who believed in me and gave me extra time and attention made all the difference. I remember a story about a university student who fell asleep in his math class. Much to his chagrin, when he awoke everyone was gone and all that remained were two equations on the blackboard. Thinking this was homework, he carefully copied the equations down and went home to solve them. When he brought his solution to the next class, he discovered to his surprise that both the equations were considered unsolvable and he had found the solution to one of them! I felt like this student because, with no formal training in the field I was embarking on, I didn't know what was possible or impossible. I approached everything from the perspective of: let's see what happens. Over time I discovered we are capable of more than I had ever dreamed possible. Possibilities and potential lie deep within us. Once the barriers are taken away and the path is clear, our true essence is freely revealed.

Dramatic changes are supposed to take months or even years of intensive therapy, treatment, hard work or coaching. Most people believe that; I did for a long time. I'm writing this book to tell you this is no longer true. Change can happen very quickly if we let it and "miracles" can be part of everyday life. I worked with my eight-year-old niece Rebecca, whose hands were covered with hives that just wouldn't go away. After a month of countless visits to the doctors and bathing Rebecca twice a night to soothe the itching, her parents were at their wits' end. My sister-in-law, a nurse of 18 years, asked if I would try and find out what was causing the hives. I agreed to chat with Rebecca; we talked for about 20 minutes. Within 48 hours her skin was completely clear and the rash has never returned.

Health isn't reserved for just the lucky; well-being is a state we can all enjoy, every day, and high performance isn't just for the elite.

If this is true, what is the secret?

When I have an opportunity to work with an individual with an illness or injury, I picture them as an energy system with an energy blockage. This blockage has a story to tell. The type of illness or the location of an injury tells me a lot about the psychological factors that have led to the symptom the client is experiencing. For example, I discovered my 10 years of lower back problems were connected to insecurity. I had a recurring ankle injury while playing baseball, and it was connected to a major decision I was struggling with. I felt either choice would result in a win-lose outcome. Once I resolved the conflict and made my decision, the ankle injury cleared up. When there are many symptoms, the picture is often even easier to read, because you can identify the pattern more easily and locate the real cause.

Three years ago a gentleman named Lloyd came to me for help. His biggest concern at that time was a speech impediment: he stuttered 95 per cent of the time. It was so bad I finally had to say to Lloyd: I don't know what in the heck you just said. You're going to have to write it down for me.

Lloyd had a list of concerns besides the speech impediment: he was seeing a psychiatrist for anxiety, panic attacks and chronic depression, and the psychiatrist had prescribed medication. He was also in the midst of losing his job and separating from his wife. All of Lloyd's symptoms stemmed from a deep sense of insecurity. The key was to find the origin of this insecurity and release the emotions that were creating an emotional "logjam" in his system. Once this logjam was released his system relaxed and the symptoms started to dissolve.

After spending three hours together on the first visit and returning for an hour-and-a-half follow-up 10 days later, Lloyd's speech impediment had decreased dramatically. In those 10 days Lloyd also began exploring a new job opportunity and he and his wife had started to work on reconciliation. His anxiety, panic and depression all disappeared.

Three months later I called Lloyd. I was doing long-term follow-up with clients, and I asked him how he was doing. He told me he was doing very well. In fact, he said, "Two weeks ago I stuttered a bit again and realized I had forgotten I used to stutter all the time." In three months he had gone from 95 per cent stuttering to less than one per cent stuttering and amazingly, he hadn't even noticed.

Lloyd had returned to what I call his natural state and, once there, stuttering became a distant memory. How did I lead Lloyd back to his natural state? First, I had to find the path for myself. It started with my wanting to overcome the pain and suffering I felt on a daily basis. I too had a grocery list of symptoms: multiple addictions, co-dependency, chronic back pain, migraines, to name a few. It seemed no matter how much I did, or what I accomplished, none of it made any difference to the pain that was inside of me. I went looking for skills and tools to deal with my pain and ended up completely transforming my understanding of myself and my world. Once I did this, I knew it was possible for others.

My skills did not develop overnight; it took 23 years and hours and hours of experimenting to filter out what did and didn't work. Over the years the process I developed evolved. I got quicker and quicker with each client, noticing what was important and what to focus on. Like a big puzzle once you've connected enough of the pieces, you can see what the whole puzzle portrays. It's even easier if you have looked at the cover of the puzzle box. In effect I have the picture of the puzzle in my mind but because each person is unique I need to see several pieces to know what I am looking for. The most important criterion to me is effectiveness, which is why I have spent so much time learning how to identify the real cause of any symptom.

Most of what I learned did not come out of a book. My self-styled 'university' evolved from resolving my own issues, working with others, and years of courses and intense training. My voyage of discovery has taken me in many different directions. When a new idea appeared I pursued it; I learned all I could about it and took it into myself. I tested it and found the parts that worked for me. This started when I was deep in my addictions and searching for a way out. I thought I could do it on my own, following the old model of self-reliance, but soon learned better. I threw myself into AA, which was a life saver for me. Once I was sober and my thinking was clear I knew I wanted more out of life. I started taking courses: Reality Therapy and Choice Theory, Neuro-Linguistic Programming, meditation – I was looking within myself and looking outside, discovering concepts and ideas. I was so thirsty to learn and grow. I continued building, integrating, exploring further; I studied Brain-Based Learning, Mind-Body connections, the nervous system, cell structure and Crystal energy; the lives of extraordinary people, the study of excellence – and the barriers and blockages that limit us. I tested all the ideas on myself and later with my clients. I was able to take all the various elements and bring them together, into one cohesive model. Every person who came to me to improve their life or performance played an important part in my 'university.' My ability to assist others so quickly today is due in part to all the people who had the faith to work with me while I was still evolving my process. And that includes people who didn't get the results they or I desired. They were my greatest teachers.

Stories, clients' stories and my stories, are the vehicles I've chosen to describe the journey I've taken. My personal story focuses on learning, change and growth – all of it powered by an insatiable curiosity. What are people like? How can they find the way to outstanding performance, unimpeded health and the inner peace that allows all their buried potential, skills and talents to flourish? How can I help them tap those rich resources, and how can I resolve my pain and anguish and develop my own potential to its fullest?

Change is at the root of it all – positive change. Don't expect to find a magic pill in these stories. One-size-fits-all simple solutions are just not what life is about. What is in this book are the key ideas that allow change to be possible. Change cannot happen if you don't know it is possible, or if you have beliefs that stop you from growing and changing. My pattern of sabotaging myself every time I would start to get ahead was rooted in some key issues I needed to resolve. As I worked on these issues I found the pattern that links all destructive behavior. This destructive pattern was like toxic waste that spoiled everything I started. Once I cleared this contamination out of my system I was like a garden with the ground all prepared for future growth – and I had lots of new seeds ready to be planted. Sharing these ideas with you is like planting another garden; it will nourish not only you but everyone around you.

The garden I envision is one that can reach around the globe. And to cultivate a garden this big you certainly need others to help and join in. To my great good fortune two of my early mentors, Lynn Sumida and Steve Davis, have joined with me, believing in the vision I have and the process that helps people profoundly grow and change. Their ability to teach others will allow this garden to flourish from continent to continent. In Chapter 11 you will read about their journeys and why they decided to join mine.

Over the years my colleagues and I have worked with clients ranging from professional athletes to Olympians, from entrepreneurs to CEOs, as well as with couples in relationships, children, and people with major health issues, some of whom the medical profession saw as incurable. This book is about triumph and change. How we can all make changes of great magnitude quickly and recognize who we truly are without the masks we have used to cover up our essence.

I want this for everyone – to help show the way, to show how, from very modest beginnings, I reached a level of peace and healing, a higher level of consciousness and openness that released constricting forces in me and freed the essence of my spirit to excel. Through the stories in this book you will see the journeys people took and what is possible for each of us. Understanding the roots of my own fears and limitations is where this story begins.

1

I don't know the key to success,
but the key to failure is trying to please everybody.
BILL COSBY

I GREW UP WITHOUT ELECTRICITY OR INDOOR PLUMBING. We lived in a cramped three-bedroom house in rural Prince Edward Island. In a poor community, we were at the low end of the food chain. We didn't have a lot. We often went to school with no lunch because we just didn't have it. We were lucky if we had something to eat for breakfast.

We did have a bread bin. All the plastic bread bags were just left in the bin. By Friday we were looking in it to see if there was a heel somebody had missed. If we found one we'd put the stale heel in hot water to make a 'bread pudding' so we could eat it.

I was the middle child of nine children. Actually there had been 10, but the first, Rita, died at six months. It is my sense that this affected Mom's relationship with the rest of us. There was an underlying fear within her: she lost her first baby and she was terrified of losing every one of us after that.

We also had religion: a really strong, strict, moralistic Irish Catholic faith. You never missed mass on Sunday and you went to confession every two weeks. If you didn't go to confession, you couldn't go to communion. If you didn't go to communion, everybody in the community looked at you like you were a sinner. If you went to communion without going to confession, you just committed a mortal sin and were going to hell; it was a closed circle. In addition to all this, I was an altar boy for eight years, which was seven more than I wanted to be.

Then there was alcohol. Alcoholism was rampant on both sides of the family. On my Dad's side, four of the five boys were chronic drinkers and one of them ended up on skid row in Toronto. My mother only had one brother and he didn't drink much, but when he did he was a holy terror.

Dad was a heavy equipment operator. He would drive the heavy equipment home in the evenings or on weekends and do jobs on the side. He was often paid in liquor instead of cash and sometimes he didn't get paid at all. On the inside he seethed with anger and resentment toward people, which mostly he handled by drinking.

Years later I could see similar patterns in me. Dad never asked for payment, he didn't value himself and what he did enough. Neither did I. The mix of poverty and scarcity was my second skin. Not just physical poverty and scarcity, it was emotional poverty too. Growing up I felt rejected, abandoned, criticized or ignored. I never felt safe.

That was how I perceived the hand I was dealt. Not that I had a clue at the time. It's like swimming: you're wet the second you are in the water. Whatever language surrounds you when you're growing up is the one you learn to speak. I learned a language of fear, scarcity and anger.

As far back as I can remember my body was tense, always on guard. I couldn't relax. My emotional pain kept me searching for answers, answers that were always outside of me, answers like: "If I were rich, it would solve everything." Of course, I discovered this wasn't true.

Today I know: Addiction issues aren't genetic. It's the thinking underlying them that is passed down from generation to generation. Years later I realized that our most destructive patterns are learned quickly and silently, not gradually or selectively. When we are young, so much learning happens at an subconscious level; you don't say: "I don't like that pattern, that attitude, I won't take it; I'll be different." Growing up, you are not really aware of the patterns coming at you and the patterns that are recorded in your nervous system.

But I'm ahead of myself.

Sometimes we have clear memories of things that happened, almost it seems before memory begins. They are signposts – telling us there is something significant we need to pay attention to. When I was about six months old I can remember such an incident. I was lying in my crib playing with my feet, feeling very calm and peaceful, when all of a sudden, a loud sound terrified me. Was it my parents fighting? I didn't know and I panicked. My mind started racing trying to find a solution. To me it was like grasping for a rope suspended in thin air, just beyond my reach. This was my first experience of panic and the need to handle it on my own. This incident clearly stands out in my mind and I wonder, could my need to control and be so self-reliant develop from a single incident like this?

The next big jolt to my nervous system came when I was three. In my family there was a great deal of insecurity; everyone had something – most of us sucked our thumbs, wet our beds, stuff like that. I had this security blanket I dragged around with me wherever I went. It was pink and I called it Pinkie.

One day my Mom decided it was time to get rid of my security blanket. She thought I was old enough not to need it anymore. In her parental wisdom at the time, she decided to hide Pinkie. But I didn't know that, I just couldn't find my blanket. For the longest time, which turned out to be nine months – I moped around looking for my Pinkie.

In our old farmhouse the kitchen and dining room were all one room separated by an archway. There was a wood-burning stove and a closet for the old paint, worn-out brooms and all the things you won't use for an eternity, but couldn't throw out because they might be useful someday. (This is a good metaphor for how most of us deal with the past. We hold onto the past and store it. Just like the paint cans, it hangs around until you properly dispose of it. But unlike the paint cans, the past doesn't stay neatly in the closet; it seeps out, creating pain, misery and suffering on a daily basis.)

One day, when I was rooting around in the closet, I found my Pinkie. I came out of that closet with every single ounce of energy you could imagine in a three-year-old. I was running around hollering, "Yeeehooo, I found Pinkie!" My Mom was sitting by the stove with a couple of my sisters while I was bouncing and waving Pinkie around, so full of joy, just ecstatic. I'd found my Pinkie.

Mom's style was usually gruff; just like a bulldog. She jumped up, grabbed me by the shoulder and said: "Give me that thing." She tore Pinkie out of my hands, ripped it up and threw it in the stove. It was all over in seconds.

Instantly I plunged from ecstasy to total devastation. I was shocked to the core. My mother, who was supposed to care for me, had tossed Pinkie in the fire. In a single second my nervous system was imprinted for the next 40 years. At three years old I told myself I'd never fly that high and fall that far again. I decided I would rather not have something, than have it and lose it. And I decided I was not going to trust anyone. Not even my mother. **These were the core patterns contributing to all of my addictions.**

Growing up, I was called Donnie. One day at age five, Mom and I had an argument. Well, it wasn't really an argument because you really didn't argue with Mom. You just shut up and took it. I was so upset on this particular day I remember saying to myself: I can't be Donnie anymore because nobody likes me, not even my mother.

Right there I made the decision to be what everyone else wanted me to be. My goal was to be accepted, which I thought meant being loved. I wanted the approval from others because I couldn't see the beauty inside myself. I started down the path of molding myself into whatever anyone else wanted me to be. I believed this would fill the emptiness inside.

But it did just the opposite. By giving everyone else the power to control the love I got, I created my own powerlessness. This powerlessness fed an even greater need to control things. It became a vicious cycle of constant internal conflict, like being tumbled in a dryer filled with rocks. My child's body coped by sending signals of distress: first thumb-sucking, then bedwetting, then migraine headaches by the age of seven.

A saving grace might have been that I was one of my Dad's favorites. Dad would take me on his trips to get firewood. He would hide me in the car so my brothers and sisters couldn't see me and I'd spend the whole day with him. It was wonderful. Or at bedtime, if we were sitting on the couch, he would hide me behind his back when Mom wanted to put me to bed. The problem was, when Mom wanted to get at Dad for his drinking, she knew exactly who to pick on. And my brothers and sisters didn't appreciate the favoritism, either. To make matters worse, Mom had her favorites too, and the favorites on both sides would go after each other. The kids were the pawns in a larger game of control. I've realized that – through all this chaos – it was Mom's inability to show me love the way I wanted to be shown love that left the strongest impression. Unfortunately even if she had shown me love, after Pinkie, I wonder if I would have believed or trusted her? But I kept trying…

I was always trying to win Mom's approval. When I was eight, I remember scrubbing the whole kitchen floor with a mop while she was in town. I had this picture in my head of Mom coming in and seeing the clean floor and being happy and excited and wanting to know who did it. I was all ready to say I did!!! Of course, I was thinking she would top it off with a big hug. And as was my pattern, my hopes were sky high.

As Mom walked in the door I was waiting with a big smile on my face. She asked, "Who mopped the floor?" I proudly announced: I did. Her response was, "Well, if you're going to do it, do it right. You missed a spot over here!" I felt so insignificant and completely devastated.

This was just one example. Often I'd light the stove at five in the morning to warm the whole house hoping somebody would appreciate me, but nobody seemed to. Many mornings I walked two miles to the store before school to get food for breakfast or lunches. Or I would wake up in the middle of the night to help Dad pull in the smelt nets. Why did I do all this and more, in spite of no appreciation – and sometimes even criticism? I didn't really know then. I know now.

Four years ago I was back on Prince Edward Island for a visit and I took my Mom for a walk along the seashore on what's called the boardwalk. I said something and Mom started to rip me apart with her cutting tongue. I calmly asked her if she was aware of what she just said, and of course she wasn't. I gently asked her some questions about what she was hoping to achieve and what she was trying to do. Then something happened I very seldom saw from Mom: tears came into her eyes and she asked me if I could explain what I was saying so she could understand and do it differently.

I took my Mom through the process I'd developed and it was a beautiful experience. As I worked with Mom, she shared the pain she felt regarding her mother. It was amazing, but not surprising, to know that when Mom was three years old, she had an incredibly painful experience with her mother, in which she felt rejected. She was still living out this rejection, in her day-to-day behavior, at a subconscious level. Tears welled up in my eyes and I was flooded with compassion for this woman who carried all this pain for 70 years. All those years she believed she wasn't loved or valued, the very same way I had felt for so many years. How ironic, Mom and I felt the same and her mother too, generation after generation, all believing we weren't loved or valued. Stopping this cycle could begin with me and I was determined to find a way out of this pattern and take ownership of my life. Even though I didn't have all the tools I have now, it was still wonderful to see some of the changes Mom made as a result of going through the process.

Mom told me a story about how, before she met Dad, she had traveled to Montreal for a vacation with some friends. She really enjoyed the travel, freedom and friendship. She loved to dress well and look good, finding ways to do this even when there was very little money. Then she returned to Prince Edward Island, fell in love with Dad and raised nine kids while dealing with poverty and alcoholism. I can only guess at the yearning she buried deep within her for living a life of travel and adventure. The sad thing is when you bury something, sometimes even you can't find it. When Mom and Dad had a chance to travel later in life, they didn't take advantage of the opportunity.

BY THE TIME I WAS FIVE MY SYSTEM WAS SO CONFLICTED I couldn't resolve even a simple problem. I stole a five-cent apple from the corner store and felt such overwhelming guilt that I spent two years trying to undo this sinful crime. Was it my Irish Catholic upbringing that left me so ashamed? Or was it simply my own conflicted emptiness?

What I knew at five was that I couldn't put the apple back because I had eaten it. Should I go to a tree and pick another apple and put it back? What color was it? Do I tell them I stole the apple? This gnawed away at me for two years. All the time I was thinking: You're evil and you're bad and you're going to hell.

Then I found the solution. At seven I went to my first confession and I felt as if I had been forgiven all my sins. Afterwards, I remember skipping down the hill from the church. I felt this ecstatic lightness, light as a feather, my heart unburdened and my conscience clear. God forgave me. It was so extraordinary. It was an unforgettable feeling against which I've measured every experience since. I realized all the pain and misery around me and in me didn't have to be there.

As ecstatic as that feeling was, it didn't take long for me to lose it in my everyday life. All the contamination inside and surrounding me leached away the lightness.

My daily lessons were a long way from forgiveness. I remember distinctly my oldest brother and my Dad standing in the kitchen pounding each other with their fists. This was the unspoken, but very real, language I was learning.

I was a bully for the first three grades of school. I fought everybody and nobody near my age could beat me. I even fought boys one and two grades above me. One day I hit a kid and gave him a black eye. Later his brother, four grades above me, met me in the hallway. He said, "Are you the one who gave my brother the black eye?" I said yes – and BAM! Just like that, he slammed me between the eyes. Blood was everywhere. That was it, I quit fighting right there. The pain was too great. After that I did everything I could to stay out of fights. On the surface this might seem like I was making progress by no longer being a bully. But underneath I was still seething and boiling. All I'd done was change my style. As a bully I was coping aggressively; as a victim I was coping passively. Fighting was a symptom, not the cause. And what I didn't know was that coping was still just coping. Bully or victim, the names didn't matter – I wasn't actually solving anything.

Living at home I learned the language my parents were teaching me. You fought, you yelled, you never, ever, felt safe. The contamination was etched into my day-to-day life. The one positive language I learned at home was hockey. The whole Smith family – brothers, sisters, cousins – were avid hockey fans. There would actually be heated arguments after a team won a special game like the Stanley Cup, or put Toronto or Montreal out of the playoffs. Growing up I always wondered if I would ever get a chance to play and to prove how good I was.

In the late '50s and early '60s, when there were only six teams in the NHL, 99 per cent of the hockey fans on Prince Edward Island were either avid Toronto Maple Leafs fans or avid Montreal Canadiens fans, there was no in-between. I, of course, picked the best team, the Toronto Maple Leafs. My favorite Leaf was Eddie Shack, a hockey player who made up for a lack of talent with sheer aggressiveness and a willingness to take more than his fair share of hits. Shack's nose looked like a ski jump hit by a mallet: he seemed to break it twice a season. So whenever we played hockey that was who I pretended to be; I loved his craziness, no cares, go-for-broke attitude.

When winter came, Glenfinnan Lake would freeze and we would skate around and play hockey for hours. Because we had no money, we always had hand-me-down skates. I had to tie the skates up with twine to give support so I wasn't skating on the side of the skate instead of the blade. Like every one of my friends, I dreamt of playing in the NHL. Hockey was the highlight of my life. Accidents were the opposite.

When I was about eight-and-a-half Dad was in a severe construction accident at the loading docks of the shipyard. The seat broke on the bulldozer he was driving and he fell off. He was caught between the blade of the bulldozer and the hull of a ship. He was very close to death for a long time. I couldn't deal with this. To protect me, I remember creating a black steel box in my mind with no doors or windows in it. Daily, I would imagine myself climbing in there to protect myself from the dangers of this world. I was so full of fear, at times it was paralyzing and this went on for many years.

I was nine when my youngest brother Jamie was born. All of the kids were sent somewhere while Mom was in the hospital. I went to my uncle's farm for two weeks. I loved being on the farm; it was fun. Toward the end of the two weeks Mom and Dad came to visit. I was out playing and never knew they had been there. I found out later Uncle Vernon told them it would be great if I could stay on the farm. I could be a real help; I could milk two cows before going to school, feed the chickens and pigs and get up into the loft to throw hay down. Mom and Dad agreed and the decision was made. That was it.

But nobody told me! I waited for Mom and Dad to come and get me.

After about four weeks I decided I would go home. That afternoon, after school, I got on the bus to go home rather than to my uncle's. My oldest brother Ivan threw me off the bus and told me I couldn't go home until Mom and Dad said so. I tried getting on that bus for three days and each time Ivan threw me off. My confusion was growing bigger and bigger every day and so was my loneliness. Why wasn't I going home? When I tried to go home and Ivan told me to get off the bus, I felt even more rejected. Why was this happening? What was wrong with me? Finally I gave up. I stayed on the farm and waited for Mom and Dad to come and get me. I waited for two years. I remember thinking that there were nine kids in my family and I was the only one not home, the only one not loved. I didn't realize that my uncle wanted me, or that my parents thought they were doing my uncle, and me, a favor. I just wondered every day if that day was the day I'd be going home.

During the two years at the farm I started repeating grades in school. I was lighting fires, stealing money and running away. Attention seeking? You bet! Years later I realized I was acting out all my previous fears of rejection and abandonment. But being left on the farm went a lot deeper. Believing I was the only one not loved in my family affected every single relationship I ever had… until much later.

The irony was palpable. When I was on the farm, for the first time in my life I had my own bedroom and three meals a day. My Granny, who lived with my uncle, bought me anything I wanted when she went to town. But I minimized all of this. I only saw my world in terms of abandonment. I focused on what I didn't have. I could not see what I did have.

Playing sports was the one way I found to get out of the mental turmoil. Our community had a local hockey team run by the Catholic Youth Organization – the CYO – for players ranging from age 13 to 21. There were 12 teams in the league. I could hardly wait to turn 13 so I could play. Even though I admired Eddie Shack, I always liked playing the nets, goal-tending. The year I was old enough to play, the league dissolved, so I never played organized hockey in my early teens. I was extremely disappointed, but I still had a passion for sports. I had natural athletic ability, which I channeled into baseball in the summer. I had a wicked right arm and could really throw the ball. However, even in sports my extreme insecurity and emotional problems got in the way.

We lived 12 miles out of town and someone on the all-star team noticed me playing in the country, with my wicked right arm, and invited me to try out for the team in Charlottetown. I went for two practices. They put me in the field and, of course, I was rifling them into home plate. Then we had a game. They put me up to bat in the ninth inning even though I hadn't played the whole game. The pressure I put on myself was so great that when I struck out, I never went back. At that time, and for many years to follow, I identified my behavior with who I was. Striking out, even once, meant I failed and that meant I was a failure.

My way of coping with any pressure was to try and fit in, no matter what. One night at a country dance, two guys asked me if I wanted to go for a drive to the bootleggers. I was so pleased to be asked I said yes, not once thinking of the possible consequences. The driver, Lenny, had a '64 Mercury sidestep half-ton with a 390-cubic-inch motor. There were no mufflers on it. On the way to the bootleggers, Lenny told me he had already downed 24 beers that day. At the bootleggers I personally watched him drink a mickey of moonshine. On the way back to the dance hall he decided he was going to scare me and the other guy. On the highway, going approximately 100 miles per hour, we passed the RCMP going in the opposite direction; they made a U-turn and came after us. Lenny decided to race the RCMP and we flew down the highway at well over 120 miles an hour. We knew how fast we were going because the police report said they were going 120, and we were going even faster. One mile from the hall, Lenny made a left-hand 90-degree turn. The instant he hit the brakes; the truck flipped on its side, with me on the pavement side, and skidded the length of two electrical poles on the highway – about the length of a football field. I'm against the door in total panic, waiting for it to rip off. When the truck stopped, the windshield was blown out, and the only injury was to the guy in the middle; he had a half-inch-long scratch in the center of his forehead. I am immensely grateful that I survived this phase of my life when others either died or were crippled for life from similar events.

IMAGINE A BEAUTIFUL, CRYSTAL-CLEAR SPRING FEEDING A
pond in a farmer's field, surrounded by brown grass, dead insects, belly-up
fish, dead frogs, and dead bulrushes. On this site 20 years earlier, a farmer
buried a barrel of toxic waste in the field, and now that waste was leaking
out, contaminating the water and ground. What would we do? Do we plant
seeds for fresh grass? Do we cultivate the ground? Do we put new fish back
in the pond? Of course not. That is dealing with the symptom rather than
the cause. That barrel of toxic waste needs to be removed so nature has a
chance to clean up the poison and return the ground to a healthy state.

For 17 years I kept burying my toxic waste – my hurt, anger, sense of
abandonment, the booze, the bullying, the fighting, Pinkie – all that
contamination buried deep inside me. It would seep out in my lack of
confidence, my migraines, failing grades and setting fires, pretending to be
anyone other than who I actually was – these were all symptoms. I needed
something. Something that would let me pretend there was no contamination. Something that would give me the confidence I needed and let me be
who I thought I was.

2

Failure is, in a sense, the highway to success,
inasmuch as every discovery of what is false leads us
to seek earnestly after what is true.

JOHN KEATS, 1795 – 1821

I STARTED DRINKING WHEN I WAS 17.

I had started going to country dances when I was around 15, in 1966. Officially there was no drinking at these dances and I went for a year-and-a-half without drinking.

The dances were held in church halls. There was a band up front and bench seats all around the dance floor. The girls sat on the benches and the guys stood at the back. Every once in a while, a group of guys would break out and walk around to check out the girls. I was trying to get up enough courage to ask someone to dance.

I would stand there panicking inside, thinking that if I went across the dance floor, I'd trip. And if I made it across the floor without tripping and finally got up the nerve to ask a girl to dance, she'd probably say no. And if a girl did say yes, then as soon as I got on the dance floor, I'd forget how to dance.

Even worse, if I ask the girl to dance and I remember how to dance and the music stops, I'll have to talk to her. But I don't know what to talk about. And how many times do I ask her to dance before I ask her home, and if I ask her home, what do I do with her when I get her there? I was running a hamster wheel in my mind, round and round. I had so many doubts about myself and so little confidence.

One night, this guy named Bobby said, "Hey, Donnie, I've got a mickey. Do you want to go outside for a drink?" For about 30 seconds I remembered all the chaos at home. There were card parties at our house about two nights a week, all grownups. They started out happy, laughter all around, and then there'd be liquor and soon there'd be fighting. All of this flashed in front of me and I said: No, Bobby, no thanks. Then, for some reason, I said: Oh, what the heck. The two of us killed that mickey because that's how you drank. I hated the taste. When we went back into the hall, the heat just hit me. It was like I was on fire. I spotted a girl, walked across the room and asked her to dance. Easy as that. And if she said no, that was okay; there was another girl right beside her. The fear of rejection was gone. I'd found the magic elixir.

All the confidence was there, except it was false. My feet were moving, I was talking, but the courage wasn't real. What I locked in, learned in those few seconds, was that something outside of me, alcohol, took care of all my fears and insecurities. I was a kid at the time and I had no idea of the toll alcohol was going to take, physically, emotionally and in every other way. It didn't matter that I was so sick my brothers had to take me home or that I passed out in the living room. Or that Mom caught me and I had to lie to her. What stayed clear in my mind was the complete absence of insecurity and the incredible feeling of confidence I had while I was drinking.

This was the start of my drinking. I kept on drinking and it was only by the grace of God that I didn't kill myself or someone else when I was drinking and driving. Many times I was so drunk I had to close one eye to block out the three extra white lines on the road. I was stopped seven times yet only charged once. I used my personality to talk my way out of things, never thinking I was going further and further down the wrong road.

When I was 19 and she was 18, I married Wilma, my high school sweetheart. We had two children, Shelly and Trevor. Shelly was born in Prince Rupert, B.C. in 1972 and Trevor was born in '74 in Calgary. We were kids raising kids, really. Amazingly, we stayed married for six months short of 30 years.

Whenever I was home we had a great time, we went camping and did fun things with the kids. But, gradually, the drinking became more important than anything else. I kept working hard and made time for my family, or so I thought, but the drinking was taking over more and more of my life. In retrospect, my time with my family was actually very limited and not very high quality.

A few years later I was driving a milk truck. My denial about my alcoholism was firmly in place and I'd almost convinced myself it was OK to steal small stuff to support it. One day a lady left two pennies in her milk chute and I took them. The next day I put them back because the guilt was just too much. My value of honesty, learned from Mom, Dad and the church, was deeply embedded. But two years later even this honesty would come second. I needed money for my drinking and I just wasn't making enough legitimately as a milkman.

I solved this problem: I found a way to steal milk. Each milkman picked up his assigned load, but I was able to drag an extra stack of milk cases from someone's load next to me. I had to load this quickly into the truck so no one would notice. Once we were out of the warehouse I would transfer the load to my buddy, just in case someone inspected my load. We alternated who stole the milk and split the bounty. I was so good at using the hook my drinking buddies called me the "golden hook." That's how I supported the drinking. Like everything I did, I did it 100 per cent. But the guilt kept mounting. I stole to drink, and drank to cover the guilt and shame. The more I stole, the more a black ball of guilt grew inside me, getting bigger and bigger. The vicious cycle continued.

Although Wilma and I were both from PEI we didn't stay there. I guess we believed the old saying: Go west, young man, go west! I had a chance at a job and we moved to Prince Rupert for two years and then on to Calgary, searching for a better life. Unfortunately, I hadn't addressed any of my problems, especially my alcohol addiction. I remember coming home from a New Year's Eve dance, and as usual I was totally wasted. I was driving a gold Dodge Challenger, my pride and joy; Wilma was sitting on the console between the two front seats and my youngest sister was by the door. When the cops put on the lights I kept driving for about 10 blocks. By the time they stopped us I had switched places with my wife. I argued for the longest time that I wasn't driving, until they threatened to put my wife in jail for obstructing justice. When it came to drinking I would do almost anything to avoid taking responsibility.

But that didn't stop me from getting arrested. I still remember waiting to be put in a cell when suddenly two guys in the drunk tank started fighting. The cops took a fire hose and sprayed everyone in the tank. I was thinking: Oh God, please don't put me in there. I got lucky and was put in a cell by myself. I felt humiliated, but it was a feeling I was so familiar with because of the shame I carried inside.

I was in a vicious cycle of either feeling shame or trying to rise above it by getting approval. I believed that my behavior really defined who I was, but I fought that. I was driven to achieve, to beat down the shame and guilt. My "drivenness" showed up most strongly in my work life. When I finished delivering milk I still had time to paint houses, plus fit in the essential drinking. I was *still* giving 100 per cent effort—just not in the right direction. All the time I was working and supporting my family I was in complete denial about the impact the drinking was having on people close to me. It is fascinating how denial keeps pace with addiction. I rationalized all my behavior with this line: "I work harder than anyone else."

But even when I had a chance to break the cycle, I didn't. A friend of mine was a plumber pipe fitter – a foreman building the Calgary Airport.

He offered me an apprenticeship as a pipe fitter. As a milkman I was making $4.35 an hour, plus all the milk I could steal. As an apprentice I would have a future and, ultimately, could make $23 an hour, but I'd have to start off making a paltry $2.85 an hour and go to school for two months out of every 12 for four years. I was too afraid and insecure to take the chance; so I said no.

Money was my measure whether I had any or not. It was always what I used to gauge my success against. Ironically, I would flip back and forth, playing either side of the coin. One minute I was obsessed with what I had and wouldn't take a risk, like the pipe fitting job, and next I would be hatching some hair-brained scheme to make my fortune. No wonder my wife felt she was on a roller coaster and no one was in control.

Two months later my friend told me he had another opening and he didn't know when another one would come up. I had to decide. That was on a Tuesday. I asked him when I'd start and he said "tomorrow." Wednesday was our day off at the milk company so technically I was free. The next morning I went to the Calgary Airport to start my apprenticeship as a pipe fitter. On Thursday I went into the milk company to say I was quitting. The funny thing is, I didn't make this decision from strength – I made it from fear; fear of losing yet another opportunity.

As a first-year apprentice I worked harder than ever. Within nine months I had a journeyman and a third-year apprentice working under me. Together we were pipefitting for five welders, when normally you keep up with two.

Two years later I was working on a condo in Calgary. It was November and really cold – 20 degrees below – too cold to work. The foreman came by and said, "We've got a job in Banff; it will last till Christmas, and I want some volunteers." I said: I'll go! I was thinking I could get away from my wife's control and do what I want – meaning drink as much as I want. So I went home and told Wilma I had to go to Banff or I would be laid off. I planned to go for two weeks, but because of my strong work performance, they wanted to keep me, so I ended up staying for two years. This is when my drinking exploded.

Looking back on my addictions, nine in total, they were all attempts to feel secure, to fill the void. To feel safe and to gain recognition. Working and drinking both helped me feel secure or at least, to forget how insecure I really was. But I was looking for security from the outside world; it was all external, and it was false. It was like painting over a wet, dirty board, hoping it would stick. It never would.

November rolled around again and there was a Christmas party for all the Banff contractors' crew. Free booze. Little did I know that was to be my last drinking Christmas, the straw that broke the camel's back. Wilma and I were the second couple to arrive. Wilma, by the way, is not a drinker; she might have a drink every third time we went out. I went up and got a tray full of drinks. I was going to get my money's worth! In a couple of hours I was good and drunk, carrying on, dancing with everybody, telling dirty jokes, the whole animalistic thing. By about midnight, Wilma had had enough and said: "OK, let's go home." "We're not going home," I said, "for one thing, there's still booze, and two, I still got my feet."

About two a.m. I threw Wilma the keys and said: OK dear, let's go home, you drive. After waiting two hours for me to quit drinking, you can imagine Wilma's frustration. So when I was done drinking and threw her the keys, guess what she said: "You don't know how to handle your liquor – you drive." Of course, rationally, this is crazy, but when you have two people caught in a never-ending power struggle, not knowing how to resolve it, you get farther and farther away from logic till there is no logic or common sense left. We had a 3/4-ton truck, a Ford, with a 460 motor and we were on the other side of Calgary. I said: "OK lady, get in, let's go."

We got in the truck, yelling at each other and I drove across Calgary as fast as I could go.

We got home, still screaming and yelling at each other. Still drunk, I drove the babysitter home, got back, screamed and yelled some more and with all the noise woke the kids up. So I screamed and yelled at them, too. Talk about a conflict. In my heart I loved all three very much, but thinking and feeling are not the same. The old repressions that had kept me tied down and not able to express love openly made my reactions more and more distorted and irrational. What the alcohol did was add fuel to the fire that was already raging.

3

It is not the mountain we conquer but ourselves.
SIR EDMUND HILLARY

THE NEXT MORNING I SAT AT THE KITCHEN TABLE WITH WAVES of guilt and shame washing over me. I was thinking: I could run and hide where no one would find me. The other thought was a shotgun… I could just end this. As crazy as this sounds, it wasn't until I was sitting at that table thinking about running or killing myself that I made the connection: it was the drinking. OK, I said, that's it, I'm quitting drinking.

It took me a long time to come to my senses, but as I look back, I can see something had already shifted inside of me. On some level I was already changing; it just hadn't reached the surface yet. A couple of months before, in a co-op grocery store, I noticed a bin of used books. I picked out two by Norman Vincent Peale, *The Power of Positive Thinking** and *Positive Thinking for a Time Like This**. I started reading them. This was really remarkable because up until then the only 'books' I read were *Playboy* and *Penthouse*.

* *See bibliography*

Five years before, I had quit smoking on New Year's, just on sheer will power. I'd been a two-pack-a-day smoker and then made a $50 bet with my old boss. That was it, I just quit. I won my bet and I never smoked again. New Year's Eve was again approaching and I decided I'd do the same with the drinking. So at midnight on December 31st, at my neighbor's party, holding a half-full tumbler of rye and coke – my favorite – I quit, and that was it. To this day I have not had another drink.

But I was pretty grumpy and hard to live with, so a couple of weeks later my wife said, "If you're really going to quit, why don't you give your brother-in-law a call. He's in the 12-step program." I said: Bullshit, I can do it myself. She said, "Why don't you just give him a call?"

The only reason I called him was the pain and misery I knew I'd caused my wife and kids. If this was what it took to ease her pain and my guilt, then I'd call him. It wasn't for any other reason. My brother-in-law came over and invited me to a meeting on Sunday.

I went to AA – Alcoholics Anonymous – meetings for three months, and it was pure hell. Without alcohol, I had no protection. I had used alcohol to deal with everything. Now, with the alcohol gone, it was like rubbing raw new skin, trying to deal with everything with no crutch. It reminded me of the time I was burned.

On one of my jobs as a pipe fitter I took apart a boiler. But the threads on a valve were rusted. As I unthreaded it, the metal broke off and boiling water shot out all over both of my hands, causing second-degree burns from my wrists to the ends of my fingers on both hands.

The nurse at the hospital put cream and bandages on my hands and told me to come back the next day. When I went back, they took off the bandages, cleaned up the wounds and put on fresh cream. I went back every day for a week, then the nurse told me I didn't need the bandages anymore, just cream. When I left, I had all this dead skin on my hands from the burns, skin that was there for protection while new skin was forming underneath. You may have guessed I'm extremely impatient. As we made the 18-mile drive home I started ripping off all the dead skin. By the time we arrived, I had all the dead skin off both hands. That night and the next day they were still excruciatingly tender to touch. Although the new skin was very sensitive, by the following Friday, you'd never know I'd been burned. It is miraculous how the body can heal. When I healed my emotional wounds it was the same, there was no need for any protection. But I was a long way from that point.

Those first three months of not drinking were like taking the bandages off. I had all this inferiority and insecurity and no tools to deal with it. I was out in the world trying to deal with everything, but I didn't have my fix to help me.

In the meantime, when I went to meetings I was scared and insecure. I felt naked without the alcohol. The room held about 50 people and I sat behind a post in the middle, hoping nobody would see me. One night they asked me to read "How It Works." I was so scared I was thinking: God, get me out of here. I was terrified. I thought everyone was judging me, the way I was judging myself. I found out later that it wasn't true. **I didn't know that in my mind, I used other people as a mirror of how I was thinking about myself.**

Three months later I was unconsciously thinking about drinking again. One evening, on my way home from work, I stopped at a red light in front of a local bar. I was staring at the Beacon Hotel sign, not thinking about all the terrible pain I had caused everyone, myself included. Instead, I was wondering where I could park. While I was sitting in this mental stupor, the light turned green. There was an 18-wheeler behind me and suddenly the driver blew his air horn and scared the living daylights out of me. I took off like a startled rabbit; breaking the trance I had been in. The moment passed. I believe a power greater than myself was protecting me at that stoplight.

Many people get into this "trance" and it can lead them right back to drinking. Unless the underlying causes of an addiction are resolved, this trance, to one degree or another, will always be there.

One night, at an AA anniversary party I was getting a piece of cake when a man named Meryl said, "Donn, you look terrible. I don't know what's going on, but you're not going to make it. I'm having a book study at my place on Tuesday night. Would you like to come over?" He only lived about 15 minutes away from our house, so I showed up, even though I was terrified. The book study was a discussion of the 12 steps it took 13 weeks to complete.

In the Big Book Study, we learned about all the steps in the AA program. In the fourth step, you write down all your fears, resentments and issues including stuff like sex. So I wrote everything down and, like the time of my first confession, I was very honest. There was nothing I didn't write down about my past.

The fifth step is telling somebody about what you have written. My sponsor Mike told me about this priest, Father Paul, who helped people with their fifth step. I arranged a meeting with him for six o'clock in the evening. These fifth-step sessions usually last two hours.

Father Paul's office overlooked the Rocky Mountains. I opened my notebook, with 28 pages written out. Everything I could think of was on these pages. I started reading, my head hanging in shame. From all of my experiences with Catholicism and all my confessions, I was expecting some sort of punishment. So there I was, reading all the things I'd ever done wrong in my life with my head down, waiting, waiting to hear the door open and Father Paul telling me to get out. I was sure he was thinking I was just a filthy, dirty person. I was thinking he had never heard these kinds of things before. But I was halfway through and he was still there, so I kept going. When I finished I just said: Well?

I was waiting for all the judgments to come pouring out. Father Paul stood up, came over and gave me a hug and said I was one of the most beautiful people he'd met. It was amazing, especially coming from a priest, whom I thought at that time was two steps below God. To hear that, from someone with authority, after all I had said – to me was nothing short of a miracle.

It was after dark when I finished with Father Paul. It was a starry night and I felt so pure. I came out of that retreat house and sat in my car on the side of the road. I was thinking: there is nothing wrong with me. I had the same pure, light feeling I had when I was seven and had gone to my first confession; the first time I had been so honest. You are supposed to say a prayer after you finish the fifth step and I did. I was so full of peace I remember thinking a Mac truck could run me over and it wouldn't matter. Before the evening began, I had all these fears of going to hell; now those fears were gone. It was quite a transformation.

There is a story titled *The Auctioneer* about an old fiddle that was up for auction. Each time the auctioneer called for bids for it, nobody spoke up. Time after time he lowered the bid and still nobody spoke up. Finally, as the auctioneer got ready to stop the bid, a man came up from the audience. He picked up the fiddle and began to play. The music hushed the crowd and their feet began to tap to the rhythm. When he finished, he gave the fiddle back to the auctioneer and the bids began. Now that the crowd knew the fiddle's real value, the price jumped higher and higher. That's how I felt after I had completed the fifth step. For the first time in a long time, I was able to see my true value, my true essence – at least temporarily.

My sponsor took me to meetings for three months telling everyone: "This is how you can look and feel, if you complete a thorough fifth step." I was his showpiece. Even though this made me uncomfortable, I knew he was just trying to inspire people to take the steps and get honest. Soon afterwards, I started taking people through the 12-step program myself. It seemed like the natural thing to do. Mom and Dad had taught all of the kids: "in giving you receive." I did that for the 15 years I was in the program.

I felt I was more on the right track now; there were so many perfectly timed events in my life that it seemed like someone was looking out for me.

It was almost like my life was in someone else's hands. For example, two weeks before I quit drinking on that important New Year's Eve, I returned home to Calgary on my Christmas break. I stopped in at my old job site to wish everyone a good Christmas. Al, the project manager, happened to be there. Later I learned he hardly ever went to the job site, maybe once or twice a year.

We chatted and he asked if I had my journeyman's ticket. When I told him I did, he said, "We had to let our foreman go a couple of weeks ago, would you like the job?" Shocked, I turned him down flat: Are you crazy? I was thinking, me, a foreman? No way.

When I returned to work after the holidays I told this older guy I worked with, who had lots of experience, about the offer. I asked him what he thought and he said I was crazy. I had to take the job. I called Al and asked if the job was still open. When he said it was, I asked: When can I start? "January 8th" was the answer. I quit drinking January 1st and started as a foreman January 8th. To me, this was a sure sign of synchronicity or outside guidance.

When I finished this first job, building a cancer clinic for the Foothills Hospital, I was asked to be the heating foreman on a 14-story high-rise. I'd been working on the project for about five months when Al called me into the office; he had a new job for me.

On his desk was a stack of blueprints: architectural, structural, mechanical, electrical drawings for an 18-story high-rise along with a rendering of the completed building sitting right on top. "Here, I want you to do this," he said, "I want you to be the general foreman, in charge of the whole job." I'm thinking: You have rocks in your head. I don't even know the difference between architectural and structural drawings. But Al knew my work ethic and my ability to work things out. He told me, "Tick off all the materials you need and all of the different jobs and tell me how many hours it's going to take."

I had no idea where to start. My old belief about my incompetence reared up; panic flooded my system and I felt like I was drowning. It didn't matter how good I was at something, when I was facing something new, I believed I couldn't do it. I asked other guys for help – what could they tell me about estimating? Unfortunately they didn't know much either. I was frozen in this state for about a week, filled with the panic, anger and rage that were masking my enormous fears and insecurities.

Finally, I just said: OK, God, this is hopeless; are you going to help me or not? I don't need help next week or next month or 20 years from now. I need help now, right now.

Within seconds a thought came to mind to look in a certain cupboard for a book. I opened up this book and it showed me how to begin. I just started writing down all the materials, working out all the hours for each of the jobs, and I came up with 18,000 hours. When the job was finally complete, it took a total of 18,500 hours. I was only off by 500 hours on a project that would take two-and-a-half years to complete.

There were many of these synchronistic happenings in my life, but I was still walking around with anxiety and panic. The reason for this, I later found out, was I had made changes intellectually, but not physically in my nervous system. I still did not know how to find the trigger that set this panic off or how to release it.

There were times on the job when I was just going to quit. When I talked to my AA sponsor he would say, "What floor are you on?" I'd say: I don't know, somewhere around the sixth or the eighth.

"Well which one are you working on in your head?" Oh, I'm on the 18th floor, I'd say. I was always thinking way ahead – not in a constructive way, but out of fear. I was thinking about all of the terrible things that could happen in the future.

I made mistakes. A lot of mistakes. One day I made an $18,000 mistake. Then a few days later, I made a $14,000 mistake. Near the end of the job, Al the project manager said, "I've never seen someone make as many mistakes as you in my entire career in construction. But you know what?

I've never seen anybody come out smelling like a rose the way you do. So keep up the great work."

One of the things I needed to clear up in this relationship with Al was an issue of dishonesty that had been gnawing away at me. When I was drinking, I stole to feed my addiction. As a milkman, I stole milk. Working in construction, I stole tools. Once the drinking stopped and I became honest with myself, I realized I just couldn't steal anymore.

I was nine months into working on the 18-story high-rise and I was a good nine months sober. I had a basement full of stolen tools – mostly from the company I was currently working for. I put all the tools in my truck and I made an appointment to see Al. I said: Al, I've got something to tell you. I'm trying to stay sober, I am in AA, and one of the things in AA is you've got to be honest and make amends to the people you have harmed.

I told him over the years I'd worked with him, I'd stolen a lot of tools. There were three or four thousand dollars worth in the back of my truck. I told him I wanted him to do whatever he thought was right. He could send me to jail, he could blacklist me with the union, whatever he thought was fair.

He responded, "I'll tell you what, Donn. First of all, I've done a lot of dishonest things in my life and I've never gone back to the people and said this is what I did and tried to rectify it. So, you take those tools down to the job site and you use them to do the job you are on. When you're done that job, you put them back in your truck and move onto the next job, because you're going to be with us for a long time, and thanks for the honesty."

I worked another year-and-a-half with Al and we had a wonderful working relationship. But after two years of sobriety under my belt, in November of 1981, I made a very big decision; I needed to go back to Prince Edward Island. Something inside was calling me back home. On the one hand this decision was exciting for Wilma, but also very scary because it was another change. Looking back, I think Wilma felt quite helpless because once I made a decision, nothing was going to change my mind. She had little say in the direction her life was taking if she was going to stay with me. Of course, we discussed the decision, but if I am totally honest, I had made up my mind and I am sure she knew that.

Because of how insecure I felt I went to see a priest at the retreat center and told him what I was about to do. He listened and replied, "Son, that's not faith, that's stupidity." I was devastated. I never expected to hear that from the priest. Here was someone, I believed, who cared about my true well-being and yet he was telling me I was crazy to listen to what was inside of me.

So here I am with a major, major conflict. On one side I have my own fears about going home, to the unknown; I've got all of Wilma's fears of leaving Calgary and the security we had built up; and now I have a priest – with all the respect I have for his advice – telling me that I am crazy to consider this idea of going home. Predicting dire results if I did. On the other side I have this strong urge to follow my passion and break away from logic and reason. Back and forth I went, faith one day that it would work out and doubt the next. This was the biggest risk I had ever taken and its impact would affect me for a long, long time.

Still, I had this strong call inside me to do something other than construction, so I gave my notice. I had finished the 18-story high-rise and was just starting a 33-story building. We put our house up for sale on the 1st of January and it sold January 28th, about two weeks before house prices plummeted in Calgary. Clearly support was coming from somewhere.

Al, of course, wasn't happy with this choice. He asked me out to dinner with his manager to check if I was absolutely sure about my decision. I said yes. But they persisted: "Here's what we want to do. We're going to make you the field superintendent, in charge of all the job sites; we'll give you your own truck and $50,000 plus bonuses. Will you stay?" I told them I couldn't. I knew I had to follow my instincts.

In April we moved home and I thought I'd get a job as the mechanical foreman building the new CP hotel in Charlottetown. This would get my feet under me and I would go from there. Well, I was in for a big shock!

Not only was I not able to get the job as foreman, I was not even able to get in the union. I was out of luck. Talk about out on a limb; I'd gone from a $50,000 job to nothing. I guess this was one way of underlining the message that I really was meant to do something other than construction. What it was I had no idea, but it seemed that a bigger force than me had a plan for my future.

4

Teachers open the door, but you must enter by yourself.
CHINESE PROVERB

WHEN WE MOVED BACK TO PRINCE EDWARD ISLAND, WE WERE making a new start, but in familiar territory. My wife and I decided that we would be foster parents. We would take kids into our home and take care of them until they found a suitable family. Meanwhile, the job situation for me was bleak; I drove a coffee truck. I just couldn't find another job. During that time I was angry with God, other people, even my family, for not helping me. I was still blaming and not taking full responsibility for my own decisions. I was constantly seeing myself as a victim.

But I loved being a foster parent. My wife liked younger kids. Sometimes we took care of babies right out of the hospital, until they went to a new home. Nine foster kids stayed with us over two years. When Mary came to our home she was nine months old. For one reason or another, I fell more in love with little Mary than with any of the other kids. She was like a little angel to me.

When Mary arrived I thought to myself, "What a beautiful little girl. She couldn't hurt me (emotionally), she's too small. I'm going to love her with all my heart and soul and every breath of my being." For nine whole months this was the most beautiful relationship I'd ever had. For the first time in my life I wasn't afraid to love.

Did that mean I didn't love my wife and children, my own children? Of course not. But I still had fears with them: fear of rejection, fear of intimacy, even with my own family. Today I realize the big changes I'd made working through the 12-step program were made mostly at an intellectual level. What I mean by this is I changed my thinking and started accepting what I was responsible for – my actions. But emotionally I was still on guard, watching and waiting for rejection, loss, pain. These fears and insecurities were still living in my nervous system and this meant slowly but surely they would creep back into whatever I did.

True, I was working on the problem at a behavioral level – I no longer drank. But I had not resolved the core issues that started me down the drinking path. Today I can clear things up in hours that took years before, because I have learned how to use the nervous system and the cellular structure. Perhaps this sounds impossible or arrogant, but I want to let people know about what can really happen. Human change happens very quickly when the nervous system and cellular system are involved.

While we were taking care of Mary, our doctor told us she had a heart murmur. Mary would need an operation at 18 months, when her system was able to handle it. The doctor assured us that after the operation Mary would have a long and happy life.

When the time came, Mary was taken to Halifax, about a three-hour drive. When they operated on her, they found she had a hole in her heart, not a heart murmur. Mary died on the operating table. I was devastated. It hurt unbelievably and I shut down. I closed my heart to protect myself from the pain and from being hurt like that ever again.

Then one day, three months later, as I was walking up the road to our house, the cloud that was hanging heavy on my heart lifted. Suddenly, a new feeling rose from the bottom of my toes to the top of my head. I didn't know what it was, what was going on, until a few minutes later: I realized I had loved this little girl with all my heart and soul for the nine months she was with us. I had never experienced such unconditional love before. For the first time in my life, I loved someone unselfishly, unconditionally. I found I had such a deep sense of gratitude that suddenly I was thanking God for giving me such a beautiful child to love for nine whole months. Mary taught me how to love unconditionally. In that instant, my grief vanished, never to return. Not only did my grief disappear, I tapped into an ability to love without fear. This was a profound experience personally, but later I realized it held the key to one of the most important issues I would tackle in my work: how to dissolve trauma. This experience with Mary opened my eyes to the possibility of completely and quickly dissolving trauma. It would be 15 years before I had the knowledge and skills to be able to help others to do this, but my personal experience was like a beacon of light guiding me.

Little Mary showed me I was capable of loving unconditionally and showed me how to do this with my own family. Instead of judging my daughter or my son's acting-out behavior, I just treated the behavior as something they were doing to deal with life the best way they knew how.

This is when I moved away from judging clients and their behavior also. The beautiful thing is when clients realize this, they open up with safety and honesty. This allows me to see the full picture, the way they see themselves and their world. When people are prepared to look honestly at what is holding them back, and then let it go, the results are dramatic and almost instantaneous. They are able to make the changes they really want in their lives.

ON THE JOB FRONT I'D BEEN TRYING TO GET WORK AT THE PEI Addiction Treatment Center as an attendant, but there were no openings. Finally, they took me on as an aftercare counselor. This was closer to a volunteer position than an actual job, but Dr. Leo Killorn, the director, said,

"Anyone with your kind of enthusiasm needs to be in our system somewhere."

Patients go into aftercare once they have completed the three-week program at the treatment center. I worked with them in aftercare one evening a week. Soon the men were all raving about what I was doing – saying how very different it was from anything else they'd experienced. They were saying how much more effective it was. PEI is a very small place so word got around; soon half the Island knew about it.

After a year of 'volunteering' I went back to see Leo and said: Listen, I'd sure like a job at the treatment center. He said, "OK, I've got a job for you, one midnight shift a week in the assessment unit as an attendant." I was guaranteed four shifts a month but I'd have to quit my day job. Here we go again, I thought. No safety net. **Every time I try to move ahead, I feel I am stepping off into thin air.** The internal conflict surfaced again: on one side I've got Wilma and the kids and a job with some pay coming in, and on the other side I have the possibility of a job that I have a passion about with even less pay. Do I risk the suffering of the people I love in order to pursue my purpose in life? Or do I stay in the familiar and the comfortable?

As poor as the wages were for driving the coffee truck, now my pay might be even worse. I only had the promise of one shift a week; understandably, it caused problems with my wife. But this was work I wanted to do and so I took the job anyway. I believed it would all work out, and in fact it did. In the nine months I worked as an attendant, I got at least 13 shifts and as many as 21 shifts a month. I felt the universe was looking after me. Every time I trusted, it turned out for the best.

My work as an attendant was never a problem; it was the hours. I worked on a seven-bed unit and a lot of my shifts were midnight shifts. Men would come in puking drunk, having seizures, or the DTs. They needed close supervision. The trouble was, once it got past 11 p.m., it didn't matter who I was talking to or what was happening – I could fall asleep.

At two or three in the morning I'd be sitting there, looking out a glass window at the ward and, suddenly, I'm sleeping. When I'd wake up – it might be two minutes or 10 minutes later – I'd be full of anxiety, worried whether everyone was still there or whether someone had a seizure. Finally, I went to the director and told him: Leo, I can't handle this anymore. It's not the job; I just can't stay awake past midnight. I am concerned about the patients.

Leo told me to hang in a while longer and he'd see what he could do. A week later he told me I could start training as a therapist, helping people address their addiction issues and guiding them through the treatment program. In those days the formal training requirements were minimal, not like today. I apprenticed under Leo and Dr. Marjorie Smith. What mattered most to them was how you were progressing through your own 12-step program, and I was doing really well. So for more than seven years I worked as a therapist and, in the process, received my certification as an International Alcohol and Drug Counsellor – The Addiction Intervention Association sets the standard and gives out this credential. But I knew I wanted additional credentials; I wanted to know more, and I wanted to go to university.

A friend of my wife's mentioned a Reality Therapy course and suggested I'd get more out of it than going to university. She knew my track record with school and felt this would be a better fit with my learning style. I will always be thankful she suggested this.

I met Rick Puteran and Lynn Sumida, the instructors for the course, and we instantly connected. We became good friends and they became an important part of my learning journey. As mentors, they were instrumental in guiding me as I set up a private practice. Lynn recalls what it was like at the beginning:

> Donn was the most reluctant student you can imagine. He walked in the door and told us, "I probably shouldn't be here. I'm really not good at this learning stuff." We said if he wanted to be there, that's all that mattered. He said, "No, I don't think you understand. I'm really not good at book learning and I never do well in these situations, maybe I just shouldn't be here." He almost talked himself out the door – almost!

Lynn, a senior instructor for the William Glasser Institute in California, was to be a major collaborator in my work in years to come. The techniques of Reality Therapy, which are applications of Choice Theory developed by Dr. William Glasser, gave me a fundamental understanding of our basic needs as human beings and how we live our lives trying to fulfill those needs. This was a wonderful foundation, something I was sorely missing. The needs Dr. Glasser described made so much sense to me.

- We need love and belonging – having people in our lives we care about and who care about us.
- We need power and recognition – being respected, feeling important, feeling listened to – this is something I missed most of my young life.
- We need freedom – having the flexibility to make decisions and choices in our lives.
- We need fun! Fun may not seem like a basic need to many people, but it is essential because it is connected to our ability to learn, to laugh and to play. If learning at school had satisfied this need, I would have flourished.

Dr. Glasser also included the need for survival in his model – the physical need for food, water, shelter and reproduction.

Understanding these needs, and using them as a framework, gave me a whole new approach to my work with individuals. It also led me to make a lot of connections in my own life. I realized that my need for my Mom's love wasn't something unusual to me, it was a universal need we all have. What complicated my experience further was that gaining love with one parent often meant losing it with the other. Being Dad's favorite meant I lost Mom's love. As a child if I didn't do what someone wanted me to do, I would be ostracized or isolated emotionally for two or three days. I was constantly trying to figure out what everybody wanted and trying to give it to them. Meeting my need for power almost always came second to my desire for love and belonging. It all made so much sense now.

On the other side of the coin, I saw some of my brothers and sisters doing the opposite of pleasing people; they rebelled. Rebellion didn't seem any more successful because they still paid a price: a different price but a price. Damned if you do and damned if you don't.

Reflecting on my need for freedom, I realized I never made decisions for myself; I always made the decision that I thought was best for other people. I wanted approval or love from others so badly. Consequently, I never really met my own need for freedom; my need for love and approval compromised that need too. Obviously, this didn't work. My needs were not met and the urgency to meet them screamed louder and louder.

We all need food, water and sleep on a daily basis. Imagine being deprived of food and sleep. Would it make sense just to drink more water, hoping it would take away the hunger and fatigue? In the short term perhaps, but what if the water supply suddenly disappears? If we are thirsty enough we will start drinking things we would never have considered – even contaminated water. When we have difficulty meeting one need, we often focus on other needs instead, in the hope that the empty feeling will go away. Consider the person who has trouble with intimacy, who suppresses it and works all the time instead. If our choices are severely limited, we will choose more and more extreme options. That's what I did for years.

Drinking alcohol was a shortcut to meeting all of the needs I craved, particularly freedom. When I was drinking I could say what I wanted, dance the way I wanted, and nobody was judging me – or so I thought. This was fake freedom. But for a long time I staeyed with it because, short term, it sure felt good.

Dr. Glasser's theory also states that all behaviors are purposeful – even the ones that look crazy. Let me say that again: All Behaviors Are Purposeful. Wow. It was incredible when I started looking for the underlying positive intention, what a person **hopes** will happen. It opened a new avenue of exploration with my clients. No matter how strange, self-defeating or self-destructive my client's behaviors might be, I now understood they were trying to fulfill a real need. Knowing this, I could suspend all judgment of their behavior and focus on the need that was not being met effectively. Forget behavior modification, or anything that focuses just on what you do. The key is to look deeper, to look for what drives the behavior. This had great impact for me, too. I was able to forgive myself more fully, as I understood the positive intention behind some of my very destructive behaviors and the powerful needs that were driving them.

Up to this point I blamed everybody in the whole world, especially my mother, for not meeting my needs. It was like I gave Mom a pitcher of water and the authority to decide when she was going to give me water and how much. I gave all my power away. I gave everyone else the power to provide love, fun, freedom and importance for me. But meeting my needs was not the responsibility of other people; it was mine.

As a result of giving away all my power I was immersed in three potent constricting emotions: powerlessness, helplessness and hopelessness. They were prevailing currents in my life, which could pull me under at any time. I call these *constricting emotions* because they close down your system rather than opening it up to its natural state of expansiveness. My constricting emotions waxed and waned but they never disappeared. I was angry, resentful and hostile to the people I thought were not meeting my needs; I always felt like a victim.

I attempted to overcome this constriction with my incredible drive to achieve. I just kept working more and more and more: doing what I was good at, which was at the root of my work addiction. As Choice Theory might put it, "When a person knows how to sleep well, they sleep more and more if they don't know how to deal with a basic need they are not fulfilling, like hunger or thirst." This is a key, for example, to understanding anorexia nervosa and bulimia, eating disorders that take over a person's life.

Understanding this pattern was extremely important in my work with addicts. Addicts have a dominant need they are not meeting, a need they have never acknowledged or met effectively. So they do something else, something they know how to do: they use drugs of one sort or another to try and meet that need. Addicts fill their emptiness in a way that, at one time, gave them the false impression that it worked. It's a crutch or strategy they are extremely familiar with and depend on.

When I had my first drink it gave me the false sense that my needs were met. All kinds of false courage, false confidence filled me once I took that drink – and disappeared just as quickly. The confidence and courage were not an integral part of me. I had to drink to feel as if I could say and do what I wanted. While drinking, all of my fears and insecurities got suppressed. I was able to have all kinds of fun, be who I thought I always wanted to be, feel completely safe, and make all the decisions I wanted to make. I made the connection: the answer was in a bottle.

This was an external solution. I could have picked food, heroin or gambling. But once I made the connection, once I believed something external was the answer, I embraced that addiction in the hope I could recapture the feelings that came with the first experience.

Using this knowledge with clients in the treatment center was very effective. A man named Bob had a serious criminal record of violent sexual abuse and destruction of property. He displayed the same pattern, over and over, for years. He'd been jailed on numerous occasions; the last incarceration was in the federal penitentiary. I met Bob when he was in a 28-day program to treat his addiction patterns. As Bob's time at the treatment center was coming to a close there was concern about how he would fare on the street. Four organizations were involved with his care – Unemployment Services, Addictions Services, Social Services and Federal Parole. The consensus was that Bob still needed ongoing therapy and it would likely take years before all of his anti-social behavior would fully be rectified. I was Bob's therapist while he was in the Center, and my boss, the Addictions representative on his case, asked if I would continue to work with him after he left the treatment center. I agreed and Bob came to see me on a weekly basis after he left the treatment center.

While Bob was in the treatment center the primary focus was on his addiction, but once he finished the in-patient program, we began to explore indepth what was underlying his addiction. Remarkably Bob and I only needed three months for him to make the fundamental changes needed. I zeroed in right away on Bob's need for love. He was starving for love and didn't know how to meet this need. Once he made the connection it was love that was missing, he was willing to clear up the issue.

One of the things I found from working with Bob was the skills and techniques I used were not as important as trust – the fact that the person trusted you. I was willing to share my life, my struggles, anything, that would help him feel safe enough to trust. I became the first person Bob trusted and as a result, he opened up to me. He was finally willing to really look at what was causing all his pain and begin releasing it. This was the pain that was driving his system and resulting in all his bizarre behavior. I helped him pinpoint a time in his life when he was rejected, in this case by his Dad, and release all the emotion locked in his nervous system from that experience. All of a sudden his system wasn't in crisis and could stop putting up barriers for protection. With this issue resolved, Bob was able to learn how to get love without fear of rejection. Once he could do that he no longer needed to act out in the extreme ways he had in the past. It was like giving him his own bottle of water; now he knew how to fill it. Five years later, he was still sober and he'd had no more run-ins with the law.

Looking at my own life, I realized that I'd never resolved my rage, which is a symptom of feeling powerless. AA didn't resolve it and neither did any of the other traditional approaches. They only made a small dent. Choice Theory started me on the path of understanding my rage in a new and different way. Before learning about how behavior works, I never knew I had a choice. Counting to 10 is useless if you have already tapped into the anger. Imagine me as a powder keg of angry feelings stored up from the past and someone throws a match. You can blow out the match before it ignites the keg, but after it is lit, it's too late. For me counting was an exercise in futility. This is no different from trying to talk a person out of a phobia when they are already experiencing it.

Choice Theory views rage as a behavior, not just a feeling. As a behavior it is made up of four parts. Think of the four wheels of a car, where each wheel represents one part of behavior. The two front wheels of the car are what we **do** and **think**. The back wheels are your **feelings** and **physiology**. Like a car they are all linked together, so if you change one, it affects the other three. If you want to change how you feel, you can use your thoughts or actions to do that – they are the front wheels; the feelings and physiology will follow.

I thought my rage came out of nowhere. I had no control over it; it just happened. Three or four times a year I would go into a blind rage and smash things. I was like a volcano with the rage building up inside until I erupted. I had no idea that thinking everyone's against me, I'm useless, bad, stupid and certainly going to hell, were exactly the kinds of thoughts that fuel those feelings. I knew when this happened I could destroy anything – even things I valued or loved, like my gold Dodge Challenger car.

I had a plastic paint job done on the Challenger. Painted up, it looked beautiful. But the door needed adjusting. I got some advice from my buddies and put a 2 x 4 in the door jamb to make the adjustment. The door moved back a bit too far and chipped a little paint between the fender and the door. Irritating, but my temper was still intact.

I made another little adjustment and the door wouldn't open at all. So I pulled on the door and it opened all right – opened and created a huge dent on the fender by the door. That's when I really lost my temper. I grabbed the door with both hands and started swinging it back and forth. I swung that door with every ounce of energy I could muster. When I finished, paint chips lay all over the ground. The fender and the door were both buckled and the door was hanging lopsided. That's how much rage had built up inside me. I had no idea how it got there, where it came from or what to do about it. I thought in this case it was the car door that created the anger, but of course it wasn't.

This pattern was a way of life for me. I had so few ways to deal with rage. It always seemed to end up with me either destroying something or getting in my car and driving as fast as I could until the rage started to recede. It was the daily accumulation of irritations and anger that I didn't know how to deal with. What I came to realize is I did have a choice, about my anger and about how my life was going, and I made some life-altering changes. The following story says it all.

In the mid-'80s CBC on Prince Edward Island decided to make a documentary about alcoholism and its effects and treatment. They interviewed a guy on skid row, an individual in treatment, and me – with 10 years of sobriety. They were comparing our three different perspectives. They interviewed my wife and me, but they also talked to my daughter Shelly, then 15, and my son Trevor, 13. They asked Shelly if she noticed any changes in me. She told them about a time when she was six and I'd taken her doll carriage from the living room and hurled it right across our street. Looking at the reporter her eyes filled with tears at the contrast. Recalling this incident and looking at me across the table, she said, "It's hard to believe it's the same person." And she was right; I wasn't that angry person anymore. Now she sees a wonderful, gentle, kind person rather than an animal full of rage.

I COMPLETED MY TRAINING IN REALITY THERAPY IN TWO YEARS and went to Cincinnati for my Certification. There I took my Basic Practicum Supervisors Endorsement, so I could guide and supervise others. Ironically, I still had a deeply buried belief that I was stupid and had trouble really picturing myself as a supervisor. My skills and knowledge were growing, but some deep constricting beliefs were still stuck within me. I didn't know how to address this problem, but I kept moving forward, trusting that somehow I would find the help I needed.

My effectiveness with addicts at the treatment center increased significantly. The training really paid off. After completing their rehabilitation treatment many people wanted to see me on a one-on-one basis. In 1991,

11 years after I quit drinking, I started working with people privately and charging a fee. I did this part-time, seeing six to nine clients regularly.

In January 1992, the same day my beautiful grandson Daniel was born, I told my wife I wanted to quit the treatment center and work on my own, full time. I would be going from a government job with a significant guaranteed income to the insecurity of private practice. I was terrified, but I covered this up with my stubbornness. My wife and I had a big fight about my decision. I knew she was worried about our security, but I was driven to move ahead. This was a pattern that created an undercurrent of conflict in our marriage. Me, wanting to move forward into the unknown, and Wilma, happy with the way things were.

My boss at the treatment center, Dr. Killorn, didn't think much of my plans either and told me so. "There's not one person in PEI who's ever paid for a service. It's all government funded. You don't have the professional credentials to be eligible for any of the funding, nor do you have the connections or credibility for doctors to refer clients to you. I'm very concerned you won't make it. I'll tell you what; I'll hold your job, and give you a leave of absence. You can come back anytime in a year if you change your mind." I said: Leo, I appreciate that, but I won't need it because I am going to make it.

Once again I stepped out into the unknown, strictly on faith. You would think I would be getting good at this "stepping out on faith," but in reality, it wasn't any easier. The pain of the present situation is what drove me to take another risk, pushing me from behind. And in front of me was this mountain of fear – fear of failure. I never felt like I was ever in a position to make a choice just out of excitement or curiosity. I always seemed to be surrounded with fear, past, present and future.

In retrospect, I think I also believed if I had a safety net, I wouldn't try as hard. So despite all the fear I did have, I took that next step. I found a 500-square-foot room for an office and hired my sister Brenda as my secretary/receptionist. Brenda was so good with people I think many came in early just to spend time with her. I also got a contract with the Federal Parole Service. As part of their parole, men who had done federal time had to work with me. All other referrals came through word of mouth because of the positive results people were having. Within a year, I had a three-month waiting list. My faith in my own abilities was paying off.

5

Man's mind, once stretched by a new idea,
never regains its original dimensions.
OLIVER WENDELL HOLMES, 1809 – 1894

I HAVE NEVER LIKED THE 'TALK AND LISTEN' OR THE 'GIVE advice' models of self-help. Those approaches take power away from the client. What I prefer to do is to keep asking questions, lots of questions. I know the answer lies within the person, not inside me. I'm tenacious; I just won't give up. I want to understand what stops a person from being all they can be. One night I was invited to a star-gazing. The Great Globular Star Cluster in Hercules known as M13 was pointed out to me. To my naked eye, it appeared to be a fuzzy star. I was amazed to learn that when seen through a powerful telescope, it actually is more than 30,000 stars with a total luminosity of more than 300,000 suns that extend about 160 light years across. I realized my questions act like that telescope: they reveal what previously was hidden, the amazing intricacy within every person.

Effective as my questions were, I still struggled with some clients who had issues that weren't being resolved. I remember one client who suffered with claustrophobia for over 20 years. She had experimented with every kind of therapy from traditional counseling to shock therapy to overcome her claustrophobia and other issues. When we first started working together, the symptoms went away – but then they all came back. After working with her for six months, I was getting discouraged.

Like this woman, some clients reverse the positive changes they make, returning to the familiar, even if it is very painful. They sabotage themselves just as they are beginning to test their wings and start to fly. Every person I've worked with, who had addictions or major health problems, had a self-sabotaging pattern. I realized that if you did not address the underlying cause for self-sabotage, you may get results, but they will be limited in duration and scope. In most of our health care systems, we see this revolving-door pattern all too often.

Self-sabotage is a conflict between the conscious mind and the unconscious mind. For example, let's say I want to be valued for my work, and I decide one way I can make this happen is to speak in front of an audience. However, if my unconscious mind thinks I am putting myself in danger by doing this – danger of being criticized or rejected – it will find ways to stop me. The range of ways it can stop me are endless; being late and missing the performance, getting hurt on the way, losing the directions. When it is in conflict, the unconscious mind can resist any change the conscious mind wants to make, using whatever strategies come to hand, even to the point of death. The old pattern is locked in the nervous system and will continue to influence our behavior and actions until it is dissolved. I realized I needed skills to help people change at the unconscious level, and I began looking for methods that would give me access to my clients' neurological pathways.

At the time I was reading three books: *Changing Belief Systems with Neuro Linguistic Programming** and *Beliefs: Pathways to Health and Well-being**, both by Robert Dilts, and *Unlimited Power** by Tony Robbins. I began

* *See bibliography*

testing some of the techniques in these books. I was able to take the client with claustrophobia through a process that was very effective. The panic she felt when she was outside her home had its roots in a very early experience. She realized that her mother didn't want her and the fear generated by this later manifested itself as a distorted perception of the outside world as highly unsafe. By pinpointing this fear, and dissolving the strong emotions it produced, this woman was able to walk around the block on her own, without panic, for the first time in 20 years.

As strange as this may seem, we had solved one problem and created another. By dissolving her fear of the outside world, an even greater conflict arose in her system. What I came to realize is that this woman was unconsciously using her fears as a way to manipulate her husband into paying attention to her. The attention she received from him is known as secondary gain. It is a by-product, but it is so pleasurable the person may hold onto the painful pattern so as to not lose the side benefits. This woman felt she had to do this because, deep down, she believed she was unlovable. This was the core issue! Because of the claustrophobia her husband showed her a great deal of attention, which she interpreted as love and affection. This made the claustrophobia that much harder for the client to give up. Resolving these issues ultimately gave my client the freedom she wanted, along with healthy ways to meet her need for love and belonging.

The techniques I used with this woman were very effective and my interest in Neuro Linguistic Programming, which is known as NLP, soared. I felt NLP offered the type of tools I needed to assist people in making changes rapidly; I could see they operate on both the conscious and unconscious mind.

I immediately went searching for more skills and the best and most accessible way seemed to be formal training in NLP. I called Lynn Sumida, who was already trained in NLP, and she recommended her teacher, Dr. Steve Davis. I called Steve and by the end of the conversation we agreed I would get a group of people together and he would come out to Prince Edward

Island and offer the Practitioner Certification program. Organizing a group was easy for me, but once I was in the program, my anxiety set in. To my surprise I still hadn't released my fear of failure. My memories and feelings connected to failing three grades in school were locked in my nervous system. Once again I was in conflict; part of me thinking: I'm going to fail again, and the other part wanting to find answers and develop skills.

WHAT IS NLP?

> **Neuro-Linguistic Programming** or **NLP** is an approach to understanding and communicating with people that resulted from studying experts such as Virginia Satir doing family therapy, Fritz Perls doing Gestalt Therapy, and Milton Erickson doing hypnotherapy. The field of NLP was founded by Richard Bandler and John Grinder who recognized that as we learn, we develop patterns (programs) that are stored in the nervous system (neurology), and are communicated in both verbal and non-verbal language (linguistic elements). NLP techniques aid people in learning new skills by discovering and employing the smallest and most easily learned elements that will enhance performance. When we are not effective, NLP helps identify specifically how we are stuck and helps locate the difference that makes a difference.

Every day in NLP training it was a battle to learn. I'd start the day eager to see what we would learn and then I'd hit a wall and everything would seem so hard. Everyone around me seemed to get it so much faster. But I forged ahead and it was worth all the "blood, sweat and tears." I learned how to help clients go back into their past and address issues deeply rooted in their nervous systems without re-traumatizing them. This was a critical skill I needed in working with clients. Many of my clients had issues from the past that were still causing havoc in the present, no matter how much my clients tried to avoid them, out-think them, or deny that anything was going on. I was also thrilled to find I was able to release many issues for myself, including my dreaded fear of failure. Addressing the past was not new for me; I had done that through the 12-step program. But clearly I had either missed some issues or not gone deeply enough. After experiencing the NLP strategies, I knew there were very effective ways to address issues from the past quickly and profoundly. What I didn't realize is how the changes have to be integrated into a person's whole system. I am a perfect example.

The day I cleared my fear of failure I developed a bulge in the middle of my back the size of a softball. This receded after a few days, but I realized later that I had been using my fear of failure to keep me from venturing into the unknown where I would feel insecure. So my fear of failure was a way of keeping myself safe. Unless we deal with the core issue that is underlying the symptom, we will create immense stress on the system and it will find other ways to handle this conflict. Once I resolved the underlying issue my creativity soared. The creativity replaced my fear of the unknown.

Often people dismiss the need to deal with the past. They want to get on with life and, as the cliché goes, "Let sleeping dogs lie." But those "dogs" are not sleeping; they are waiting for a chance to jump up and bite their owners. Unresolved issues from the past can poison every aspect of life until they are dealt with.

Let me give you an example. When my mother tore my security blanket Pinkie out of my hands and threw it in the fire, I experienced a lot of things: the initial ecstatic joy of finding Pinkie, then devastating loss, betrayal, abandonment, rejection – all in a few short seconds. I experienced them on a conscious level, and locked them in at an unconscious level. I made an instant decision never to allow myself to feel that level of joy again! In my adult life it took me a long time to realize I had placed this limit on myself, just like a governor on a car, where I only allowed myself to feel a limited amount of joy. Once I realized this I started connecting all of the dots of past experiences, recognizing the emotions that linked them. I traced those emotions to Pinkie, and then released the constricting emotions of that experience. I had thought about the Pinkie story hundreds of times and analyzed it to death, but I needed to deal with the emotional impact at the source – at the neurological point where it had been wired into my system – in order for it to be fully released.

Thanks to the NLP training I now had more of the tools I needed and I had lift-off. I could help people address past issues, resolve them in their nervous system and they literally took off. Some clients felt free for the first time in their lives. They were flying, and I was flying, too.

The wonderful thing about this experience was once I was off the ground I could see further, I could see patterns and my creativity soared. Think about walking through a forest where you can't see a way out. All you see is what is in front of you, trees and more trees. It was the same for me with clients. From the ground I couldn't see all the patterns that were present in their life. Once I knew how to "fly" I was able mentally to reach a higher plane and I could see so much more. People's symptoms are like the trees in the forest and now I could see beyond them. I started to look for patterns in all the clients who came to see me, rather than focusing on isolated incidents.

In the early '90s a client came to see me about her panic attacks. She had gone to her doctor and he told her the bad news was that she would continue to have panic attacks for the rest of her life; the good news was that she was not alone, millions of people have them. His only solution for her was medication. She wasn't happy with this answer and that is why she came to see me. The medical model, for the most part, addresses only the symptoms and in many cases uses medication to minimize the symptoms. In the initial stages, until what is creating the panic is addressed, medications are helpful, but the problem is they can mask the real issue. The symptoms are very important; they are like signposts telling me where to begin looking for the underlying cause. This is the way I worked with myself. Whenever a symptom would appear I would go looking inside myself for the deeper cause because something in our system is trying to get our attention and it won't stop until we listen. If we refuse to listen, it will shout louder and louder creating more serious symptoms or manifesting new symptoms.

So I asked this woman with the panic attacks about her history. She said she had only experienced two panic attacks, one a month earlier and one a year before. For anyone who has not lived through one, a panic attack is an incredibly intense fear, based on anticipating something terrible happening in the future. I knew these feelings because I had experienced a panic attacks on numerous occasions.

Together we began to look more closely at what was really happening in her life. Here was a lady in her mid-50s who only **noticed** two panic attacks – but she had a long history of anxiety, a history she had been completely discounting. Anxiety is a milder form of a panic attack – a fear that something is going to happen that you are not going to be able to handle for whatever reason. What I was looking for was what created that fear.

In this client's case the cause of her fear went way, way back to just after her birth. She had an experience where she didn't feel safe. This is where the fear started and it just kept building over 50 years until it evolved into panic attacks. That early experience created the perception that her world was unsafe.

My own experience of being startled by a loud noise, when I was about six months old, started my pattern of self-reliance, resulting in my noticing what's wrong, thinking the worst, and generalizing it to every aspect of my life. The Pinkie experience added another layer of anxiety, limiting the joy I could experience, setting the patterns of fear of abandonment, intimacy and rejection. The first time I failed a grade at school added another layer. I could see how all these experiences were layered, one on top of each other, but the amazing discovery I made later was they didn't have to be dealt with, layer by layer. I found a way to dissolve the first layer, and like layers of paint, all the rest fell away.

Most patterns start before the age of reason; for most of us this is before the age of five. We may not have a clear memory of what happened, but our nervous system is so accurate in recording information we cannot fool it. This allows us to track very precisely where traumas are located. Once a pattern is coded into our nervous system, it remains until the system is taught to respond differently. It keeps sending us the same message until we clear up the emotions around the original experience and the pattern it creates.

For example, in 1978 I bought a 1976 Pontiac Grand Prix LJ, fully loaded. It had everything, was in mint condition, plus it only had 20,000 miles on the speedometer. The owner never drove it in the winter. I paid the man his money and left. Fifteen minutes and five miles later, a lady cut me off and removed the whole front end of the car. This may seem like an "accident," but I realized there was more to it than what appeared to be happening on the surface.

Today, I understand how I attracted that situation. As hard as this may be to believe, I know it to be true. Losing something I really valued reflected my early pattern of feeling unworthy of receiving good things. I made sure I either didn't get what I wanted, or if I got it, I did everything to make sure I couldn't keep it. I know as I write this it sounds crazy. Here is a man filled with longing for things and yet whenever he gets them, he finds a way to mess up. This pattern of self-sabotage is typical of addicts. It also often shows up in major health-related issues. Unless the pattern is reversed, we will have very little success in making progress, no matter how strong our pictures of happiness are or how hard we work.

But once these self-sabotage patterns change, it is extraordinary how the addictions or other symptoms disappear. Are addictions hereditary? NO. What is passed down from generation to generation is the thinking that creates imbalance in the system. Just like getting wet as soon as you are in the water, you are affected, from the moment of conception, by the thinking of the people around you. The imbalance in the system creates an unquenchable urge to fill the emptiness that people experience with an addictive substance. The addiction itself is not passed down. Yes, you can have a biological predisposition to something, but it is only a predisposition, not a direct cause. We all have a unique genetic makeup: some of us have curly hair and strong stomachs and others have great eyesight. But what we do with our basic physiology is up to us. Can addictions really disappear for good? Yes, they can and do. The key is to address the underlying patterns that create the imbalance.

POSITIVE ADDICTIONS

I began to notice a change in how I was thinking about my alcohol addiction. My sobriety was quite solid and I realized the AA philosophy was linked to a pattern of thinking that I had outgrown. My thinking had been based on fear that went something like this: "You can't stay sober on your own, and if you try, you are going to get drunk again." It was a self-limiting loop.

Each AA meeting begins with introducing yourself as an alcoholic. So I would say: Hello, my name is Donn and I am an alcoholic. One day I realized I wanted to say: My name is Donn and I am very grateful I have **recovered** from alcoholism.

My thinking was people recover from other diseases, why can't someone recover from this one? Now the problem with this is it doesn't fit the AA philosophy. AA sees alcoholism as a disease from which there is no real recovery – "once an alcoholic always an alcoholic." If you think you've recovered, you will start backing off from meetings and before you know it, you are beginning the slide back into drinking. Thinking you are recovered could also be the first warning sign that you are headed towards a dry drunk.

A dry drunk describes the behavior of someone who isn't drinking, but is using all the old ways of coping. In a dry drunk, a person can be as mean and difficult as ever, but they aren't drinking. Working for years as an addiction therapist, as well as many years in AA, I met people who used the program to hide, so they wouldn't have to look at the issues underlying their addiction patterns. Their attitude was: "I have quit drinking, what more do you want?"

People who live with someone in a dry drunk sometimes wish the person would go back to drinking because they would be easier to live with. A person in a dry drunk can also be a person who is not drinking but is just inches away from starting up again. This is where I was when I sat in front of the Beacon Hotel when the 18-wheeler came along and blew his air horn, and scared me out of any thoughts of drinking. At that time, I was a long way from solid in my sobriety. I would never have survived without AA then. But after 15 years of sobriety, it was a very different story. The change in my thinking was a real statement of inner strength and a step I needed to take.

Weaning me from AA was extremely difficult given the AA message: leave and you'll go back to drinking. It took me well over a year to prove to myself that I wasn't in a dry drunk or trying to sabotage my recovery. Instead, due to my growth, I was breaking away from my sponsor, the meetings, the philosophy of being an alcoholic and the belief that I would have this addiction for the rest of my life. I was evolving beyond traditional ways of viewing myself and my world.

The concept of a positive addiction was new to me, but when I read Dr. Glasser's book *Positive Addictions**, I could see how it fit. After quitting alcohol I quickly replaced drinking with all sorts of addictions, some of which were 'positive' addictions. To be honest I had more than nine addictions, but here are the main ones.

The **first** was smoking. I smoked one-and-a-half packs of cigarettes a day and, if I spent more than a few hours in the bar, it would be two packs. I am still amazed that I was able to quit smoking, five years to the day, before I quit drinking.

The **second** was pretty obvious: alcohol.

The **third** was prescription drugs – mostly pain killers and muscle relaxants.

The **fourth** was my work; I was driven to succeed, to be better than everyone else at what I did.

The **fifth** one was my co-dependency or addiction to the relationship I was in.

The **sixth** was approval. In following my story you may have noticed that I would do almost anything to get the approval of others; once again I needed approval to fill the void inside me.

* *See bibliography*

The **seventh**, as both my children would laughingly attest to, was buying. If I had the money with me, it didn't matter how many of this or that I had at home; I would buy it anyway and worry about how I was going to pay for other things later. Some people refer to this as Retail Therapy – a way of coping with stress.

Dr. Glasser's book refers to the next two as positive addictions, but to me any addictive behavior says something is out of balance in a person's life.

The **eighth** was religion. I went to mass every Sunday, out of fear of going to hell, the mortal sin I would commit if I didn't. But in 1982 I began going to mass **every day**. This obsession lasted for two years. Now, going to mass on a daily basis is not necessarily an addiction, but for me it was, because it was driven and fear-based.

The **ninth** was Alcoholics Anonymous. I want to be clear about my appreciation for AA. In all likelihood I would be dead right now if it weren't for that program and the people in it. But the addiction part was working the program day and night just to keep going. Again I was missing the balance.

Ironically, in my religious addiction, I was accused of not having enough faith, and in my AA addiction, I was accused of **not** working the program enough. When I left these practices behind, I knew there was something beyond them, and they were just stepping stones on the path to a healthy and balanced life.

Once I felt stronger and I was able to *fly* in my professional life, I wanted my relationship with my wife to expand too; I wanted us to be able to soar together. But we had internalized so many negative patterns from the past, we were stuck, mired in the mud. I understood that much of my behavior had contributed to us getting stuck; I just didn't know how to free us from these constricting patterns.

IMAGO RELATIONSHIP THERAPY

Once again I was searching, researching, trying to find more answers. I happened to be speaking with Lynn Sumida and she recommended the book *Getting the Love You Want** by Dr. Harville Hendricks. Lynn was an owner of a very successful private practice and her firm dealt with a lot of couples and families. She said Harville Hendricks was addressing relationship patterns in people's lives, and I was instantly interested, both personally and professionally. Even though my relationship with my wife had a lot of room for improvement, I seemed to be quite good at helping other people with their relationships. I was doing a lot of work with couples and Dr. Hendricks's training sounded very impressive. I found out he had a weekend workshop for couples in New York. I wanted to try it out and my wife was willing, so off we went.

We took the weekend workshop and on Sunday afternoon I met privately with Dr. Hendricks. When I inquired: What's the chance of me getting trained in your model? – he asked what education I had. I told him about my certification in Reality Therapy as a Practicum Supervisor, my status as a Master Practitioner in NLP and my certification as an International Addiction Therapist. I also explained I had a private practice and had great success in working with couples.

He said, "No, no, no – what formal education do you have?" I told him I had a grade-12 equivalent. "What in heck is a grade-12 equivalent?" he asked. I told him it's when you don't formally complete grade 12 and you go to trade school. And he said, "Why don't you just stop right there; this would be a complete waste of time. Anybody who's taken this training has a formal degree in psychology, psychiatry or some other field; they've got masters' degrees or doctorates. Donn, you're going to be a fish out of water. Why don't you just save your money?"

But I wouldn't take no for an answer. Finally, he said, "Well you are persistent. I'll tell you what: you go back to PEI and get seven endorsements from people with some sort of qualifications and I'll decide." So I did; I got the endorsements and sent them off.

A few months later Harville Hendricks called me himself, "Donn, if

* See bibliography

72

even half of what these people are saying is true, I'd be a fool not to give you a chance." I was ecstatic and could hardly wait for the program to begin. Off I flew to New York and then bang – here comes my fear. I thought I had taken care of it, but clearly I hadn't. Just listening to the participants list all their credentials was enough to make me want to run back home. One of them had two doctorates – a doctorate in theology and a doctorate in psychology. What in the heck was I doing here? This seesaw effect went on for the full two years of the program. A few of the participants, once they heard about my lack of credentials, began to ride me very hard. I was used to this and the street fighter in me came out.

My Mom could be a street fighter too. I remember the day a neighbor came into our home with a gun. He was a very disturbed individual and when drinking was a very violent person. He had intimidated other neighbors in the past with guns and rifles. This experience was terrifying for all of us, including Mom, but she handled it very differently than we did. We all ran for cover, but Mom went right up to him, grabbed the gun from his hand and told him to get out of our house and never come back.

I finished Harville's training, along with 18 people from all over the world. When we finished we heard that two people hadn't passed. Nobody knew who they were, but I knew that I was the only one who didn't even have the credentials to get in the program.

On the last day they gave out the certificates. Finally they were down to the last three people in the course, myself and two others. Then Harville called "Donn Smith." I was overjoyed! I went up and said: Harville, thank you very much for stretching the requirements and letting me in this program. He said, "Donn, I did a lot more than stretch, but it was worth every bit of it. Come here"– and gave me a hug.

After taking the Imago training, I was able to see clearly how we attract our partners. Our partners become mirrors for us so we can see the issues we have not resolved. These patterns are mirrored back to us – by partners, employers, friends and even our children – until we resolve them. For example, if we are not standing in our power, we will constantly be bombarded by people who try to take our power away. The worst thing we can do is to blame them. What's needed is to recognize what isn't in alignment within us. Once we address this, the conflict dissolves; the power struggle is eliminated.

IMAGO RELATIONSHIP THERAPY

Imago Relationship Therapy, originating in the partnership of Harville and Helen Hendricks, integrates insights from major Western psychological systems, behavioral sciences and spiritual disciplines into a comprehensive theory of primary love relationships. Developed from the exclusive study of couples, it presents an approach that builds on and extends previous efforts.

The "Imago" is a composite image in the unconscious that holds the significant character traits and behaviors of our primary caretakers in childhood. By pairing us with an *Imago match* – an individual who is like our caretakers in emotionally significant ways – our unconscious drives us to recreate our childhood psychological dynamics in an attempt to heal the central wounds we carry. Imago Relationship Therapy is aimed at using this context to transform relationships into a therapeutic encounter, nourishing each partner's psychological and spiritual self-completion.

The challenge I met with Dr. Hendricks, of getting my foot in the door without traditional credentials, was only one of many I had to deal with as I learned new methods. I remember questioning Dr. Glasser about Choice Theory. He believes we have five genetic needs: the need for love and belonging, power, freedom, fun and survival. One day I went to Dr. Glasser to discuss this and said: Bill, I think there are two other needs that you're not addressing. He asked what they were, and I said psychological safety and spirituality. He nodded and replied: "Is that right? I'll tell you what, Donn; you can talk all you want about that, in any detail you want, just don't call it Choice Theory."

I came up against the same reaction when I was training with Eric

Jensen in Boston, on Brain-Based Learning techniques. He was talking about treating kids with attention deficit disorders and making changes using 'whole brain' exercises. I spoke up: Eric, when kids come in with those symptoms, I see the symptoms as just a reflection of a core issue. When I help them deal with the core issue, the symptoms disappear. He said: "Do you have research to back that up?" I told him the only research I had were my own before-and-after results. Dr. Jensen said that was not enough; I needed controlled studies to document the results. Although I was frustrated with this answer at the time, I started documenting the results people were getting and, ironically, that research contributed to this book.

Brain-Based Learning introduced me to fascinating ways to use both sides of the brain simultaneously, rather than using just the left side that focuses on analytical, mathematical, procedural abilities, or the right side that governs spontaneous, random, creative abilities. Whole Brain Learning is the act of putting both sides of the brain to work at the same time.

What I really appreciate about the brain-based learning research is that it supports so much of what I've discovered for myself. I knew learning involved both the conscious and unconscious and that's why I wanted to work on both levels. In addition, I was a living example of how fear inhibits learning and when you remove fear how creative we can be. And finally, I accepted the principle that emotions are critical to patterning, that emotions are the key to how information is stored in the nervous system. This was exactly what I had found when working with trauma.

BRAIN-BASED LEARNING

Brain-Based Learning Theory is based on the structure and function of the brain. As long as the brain is not prohibited from fulfilling its normal processes, learning will occur. Every person is born with a brain that functions as an immensely powerful processor. Traditional schooling, however, often inhibits learning by discouraging, ignoring or punishing the brain's natural learning processes.

The core principles of Brain-Based Learning state that:

- Learning engages the whole physiology.
- Emotions are critical to patterning.
- The brain processes the whole and parts simultaneously. Learning involves both focused attention and peripheral perception.
- Learning involves both conscious and unconscious processes.
- Learning is enhanced by challenge and inhibited by threat.
- Feedback works best when it comes from reality, rather than from an authority figure.
- People learn best when solving realistic problems. The best problem solvers are ones who laugh!

This summary is adapted from the Brain-Based Learning web site:

http://www.funderstanding.com/brain_based_learning.cfm

6

Do not go where the path may lead:
go instead where there is no path and leave a trail.
RALPH WALDO EMERSON, 1803 – 1882

I FINALLY SAID TO MYSELF: OK, ENOUGH OF LEARNING OTHERS'
models. It's time for me to spread my wings and start to fly solo. Other
people's models have really been helpful, but I was ready to develop a model
of my own, combining everything I know with what I've found that works.
**That was the moment I knew I wouldn't be using any one approach by itself,
but rather I'd be creating something of my own.**

I wove everything I knew together into a new process I called the
Metamorphosis Model. I chose this name because I saw how the process
was transforming people's lives, like the caterpillar into the butterfly. What
I did was extract the nuggets from each of the models I'd studied and I then
wove these insights together, in a way that was much more effective than
anything I had previously learned. This was 1994 and I was very excited about
the model I had so far; later, I would continue to refine the model.

I happened to be speaking with Steve Davis, who trained me in NLP, and mentioned I'd developed a model of my own. I expected disbelief and a fair degree of skepticism, given the struggles I'd had in learning and integrating the NLP material. I worried that he would think I was egotistical – who was I to think I was smart enough to create my own model? He surprised me with his enthusiasm and curiosity, asking me what I was calling it and offering emotional support.

So I began to test the model I had developed. I was my own guinea pig and my sister Brenda, who worked with me, was next in line. If a new technique didn't get the results I was looking for, I wouldn't use it. I kept the strategies that worked really well. My filter was **results**, pure and simple; because no matter how good someone says a new technique is, if I don't see the results, I'm not interested.

I used myself as the measuring stick and I looked at the results I was or wasn't getting. I still hadn't shifted some of my anxiety, my fear of failure drifted in and out depending on the situation and I had too many highs and lows. I still allowed external things to affect me and a stack of bills was all it would take to really get me going. On numerous occasions I said: I give up, that's it, I'm packing it in. It just seemed too hard. And, of course, I brought God into it, too. If God didn't want to help me, I wasn't going to do it!

Then I would have a good day and my perspective would shift: it was worth it. The roller coaster ride continued. The biggest pattern that hadn't shifted was my self-sabotaging pattern. It was alive and well and so strong that any change I made either didn't last or seemed to be such a small step that it was going to take forever to alter the pattern. There had to be an answer, and I was determined to find it for myself and for others.

At that time I already had a waiting list of clients. I began to test my new process with clients, myself and six other people who were willing to be guinea pigs. I thrived on highly resistant clients, those with addictions, serious health problems, and clients with issues I'd never dealt with before. I was testing ways to help people make changes and stop reversing the gains.

One of my challenges was Sanja, a 15-year-old student in grade nine. I worked with him because of his Attention Deficit Hyperactivity Disorder (ADHD), which his mother told me was the worst case on record on PEI to date. His mother was a school teacher; she had kept all his records from as early as kindergarten. Sanja's ADHD was so severe and his behavior so unpredictable he had to be driven to and from school in a taxi; if he rode the school bus, he was bound to get in fights.

For years his report cards were blemished with teachers' comments noting his poor academic performance and worse behavior. He was often aggressive and demonstrated great difficulty focusing on classroom work. His mother was desperate, having spent five years taking him from expert to expert, searching for a solution. I really identified with Sanja, his failure, the acting out, the emotional pain and the labels that were getting in the way of seeing the beautiful person he was inside.

When I think of Attention Deficit Disorder, I think of a person who sees multiple, rapid and simultaneous images in their minds, like watching nine TV screens all at once. They have strong emotional and physical responses to these images. The experience of overwhelming thoughts is combined with the helplessness of believing they can't control any of the thoughts and feelings. These images are the result of very strong, emotionally constricting experiences, occurring early in their lives, and not from a genetic deficit.

I worked with Sanja for three months, using the Metamorphosis Model, with seemingly little or no results. I tried everything I knew and was surprised that nothing was working. During that time Sanja was on Ritalin. His mother took him to the doctors twice to have the dosage reduced, but both times they increased the dosage instead. When three months had passed, I told his mother I didn't think things were working. Inside, I truly felt the Ritalin was interfering with his progress, but I was not a medical doctor and so I couldn't recommend that Sanja stop the Ritalin. Sanja's mother, on her own, made the decision to take him off the

Ritalin. When he came back one week later, all the work we had done together had taken effect and his behavior was markedly improved. Once he was off the drug, his system was able to integrate the new learning at a cellular level without the interference of the medication. This was a powerful learning experience for me about how our system works and how outside chemicals can interfere with the body's natural functioning.

What I felt intuitively has now been explained by research. Dr. Peter Breggin, author of *Talking Back to Ritalin**, has publicly addressed the effects of Ritalin on the brain. He says, "Ritalin 'works' by producing malfunctions in the brain rather than by improving brain function. This is the only way it works. Short-term, Ritalin suppresses creative, spontaneous and autonomous activity in children, making them more docile and obedient, and more willing to comply with rote, boring tasks, such as classroom school work and homework."

A year-and-a-half after I started working with Sanja, he and I were interviewed by the Charlottetown newspaper *The Guardian** to discuss Sanja's remarkable changes. The newspaper reported: "In under two years Sanja's average has leapt to nearly 80 per cent overall, from a discouraging 35 per cent median and he won an award for the most improved student in his high school." Sanja's progress is even more significant when you consider that he achieved the 80 per cent in a regular class, while his 35 per cent score was recorded in a special 'stay in school' program. Sanja's mother says, "We tried a lot of other people… and nobody could deal with ADHD. Nobody, that is, until Donn Smith happened on the scene."

Sanja and I spent about 35 sessions together, spaced over a year. It took that long before I was able to identify enough of the key pieces for Sanja to maintain the shifts he was achieving. Today, with my current knowledge the process might take as little as five to seven hours! What a difference honing my knowledge and skills has made to my process. But those results belong in the future. Meanwhile for me the present kept getting more and more challenging.

* See bibliography

I have never understood people who "rain on someone else's parade" – and yet that is what was happening because of some of my clients' success. It didn't make sense to me why anyone, especially a helping professional, would refuse to celebrate a person's success. Word was spreading and my clients were talking about their results and challenging some of the professionals they worked with previously. They were demanding better care. Unfortunately this caused a stir. Some counsellors went so far as to suggest the clients' results wouldn't last, and that in a year they would be telling a different story. I really felt this was a shame and it also further accentuated my aloneness. I was working in what was considered a non-traditional way, but I very much wanted to be part of a community of people dedicated to helping others.

While working with Sanja and trying to get the support of the medical profession in terms of reducing his medication, I also felt very alone in what I was doing. There was so little support from established systems and it often seemed like other professionals were creating roadblocks rather than trying to help each other.

Another story comes to mind of a woman whose brother was in a psychiatric hospital because he was suicidal. In fact, she said he was so suicidal they weren't sure what to do with him. She was walking by my office one day and saw my sister Brenda. They started chatting and the woman asked if I would see her brother. I was quite leery but agreed, on the condition that she got permission from the psychiatrist for her brother to come to my office. I didn't want to step on any toes! To my surprise she got permission, and I spent an hour with this fellow. He returned to the hospital feeling so much better that they released him the next day to outpatient care. I saw this man for a total of four hours and when that time was up, his psychiatrist declared that he was fine and didn't need any more appointments.

Looking back, in some ways I must have been out of my mind to consider this client. If this client committed suicide, my reputation would definitely have suffered; he had already been assessed as a serious risk by the psychiatric community. Why did I take him on? It was purely a response to the desperation I heard from this woman. All my life I've been driven to help people in pain. Now that I had tools that really made a difference, it was hard for me to say no.

What did I do that was so different from traditional counseling? At that time I was using the NLP technology to look at the client's 'timeline.' Our timeline describes the way we represent the past, present and future as we think about our lives. This highly suicidal client had no sense of purpose or perceived future. His timeline ended at the present. Every person I have worked with, who has suicidal tendencies, sees little or no future. Once I discovered his timeline had no future, I began to explore the reasons for this and how to bring the future back into focus.

I helped him shift the submodalities that were an essential part of how he was viewing his life. To describe submodalities and how vital they are, I'd like you to think of your senses. Imagine life without the richness of the senses, as a black and white photo, with no sound, sense of smell or taste. How exciting or interesting would life appear to you? This is what it was like for my client. If you were to think of a time when you were very excited and passionate about life and then think of a time when life lost its excitement, you would likely notice many differences in the submodalities, like richness of color, clarity of image, sound, taste or touch.

Changes in the submodality structure of his thinking had a dramatic impact for this client. Life suddenly seemed worth considering. Our three other sessions, after he left the hospital, involved transforming core beliefs, which had created the hopelessness and despair to begin with. Two years later he sent me a postcard from the U.S. saying how well he was doing and that he'd never had a recurrence. He was also now busy at a job he enjoyed immensely.

You might think the results with this client would have created interest in what I was doing, or at least some appreciation for it by the helping professions, but that wasn't the case. It was almost the opposite. I was truly surprised at the lack of interest in a new process that could help clients. The ray of sunshine came when I met a doctor of internal medicine. He was a doctor who truly wanted more for his patients. He believed they could and should get better care. We were a perfect fit. He was the first person in the health care system I felt was speaking my language. We had similar ideas about change and he was open to personally experiencing anything he recommended for patients.

Personally, he suffered from Seasonal Affect Disorder or SAD and had been on Prozac for seven years trying to deal with anxiety and other issues. He promptly agreed to try the Metamorphosis Model. In his words: "I had my own issues, as everybody does. I think 90 per cent of the population has neuroses. I read that a university professor claimed he never met anybody who did not have unconscious traumas locked in their nervous systems. I had problems with depression and a lot of anxiety. Through my conversations with Donn, I decided to undertake his training to see if what he did was of value. Donn has incredible confidence in what he is doing. He is really kind and gentle, soft and accepting.

"I had some very powerful experiences; I would call them spiritual experiences. I don't know how else to categorize them. As a result of Donn's work, a lot of energy started moving in my body, with deeply felt sensations of love and healing. I found afterwards I had no problems with anxiety and depression."

The doctor phoned me 10 days later to say: "Donn, I've got all kinds of people I want you to engage in this process to see what is effective." Waves of emotion swept over me when he said these words. Finally there was someone who could see the value of what I was offering and wanted to work with me so the Metamorphosis Model could become mainstream. He continued, "One person has chronic fatigue and fibromyalgia, one has insomnia, another has an attention deficit disorder and on and on. Let's see how they like it. I want to know what kind of results they can have. I know we both have a tremendous desire to shift the pain, misery and suffering in people's lives."

This doctor had been frustrated for a long time by the lack of effective psychotherapy available to patients and he had been searching for answers on his own. He connected with researchers at Harvard, who were studying the use of cognitive behavioral strategies to help people reduce their risk factors for disease, as well as to identify how diseases have a mind/body connection.

When he was introduced to the concepts of Eastern philosophies and Eastern medicine, he became fascinated with both. We had similar ways of looking at the world. "Not all of the health problems start with biological faults in our DNA or accidental exposure to toxins or bacteria. Most originate around lifestyle and stress, the choices we make and the positions we place ourselves in," he said.

We were both interested in creating a Wholeness Center that would address these different philosophies of healing. He and I quickly started gathering research material in the hopes of opening a Center on Prince Edward Island. We even had a farmer willing to sell us one of the most beautiful pieces of property on the Island, 56 acres, for $120,000. We figured we were on our way. We gathered together a group of 18 people – architects, doctors, lawyers, nurses, counselors, engineers, managers, marketing people and strategists – to discuss the project. There was lots of enthusiasm, but as time went on and the excitement settled, only three people were really willing to make this project happen and the biggest challenge for the Wholeness Center was, of course, money. We didn't have any. People were willing to help, but the bottom line was I would have to find the money. So I came up with the idea of going on tour to raise interest and awareness of what the Metamorphosis Model had to offer.

Just before I left PEI, I received some very encouraging news. Bradford Associates, a local firm that conducted social research, had examined my model and found it had an 85 per cent success rate. Bradford Associates researched the issues people identified at intake and their stated outcomes to measure success, collecting their data through interviews with clients.

When I left Prince Edward Island in September 1996 for the tour, my goal was to raise interest and support for the Wholeness Center. I had speaking engagements across the prairie provinces, Manitoba, Saskatchewan and Alberta. I wanted to interest people in going to PEI to experience the Metamorphosis Model, and to find professionals who wanted to work with us at the Center. I hoped that, coupled with the doctor's support from a medical perspective, there would be enough interest to build this Wholeness Center. But generating interest was much harder than I had anticipated. After making my way across the Prairies, I found that lots of people were intrigued with the process, but few of them wanted to travel all the way to the east coast of Canada. Gradually it sank in that perhaps I'd bitten off more than I could chew.

7

Wheresoever you go, go with all your heart.
CONFUCIUS, 551 – 479 B.C.

ON MY TRIP WEST I STOPPED IN CALGARY TO VISIT FAMILY AND met a gentleman who was president of Ikon Office Solutions there. We began talking about what I did and the results I was getting. He told me there was no way that I could get those kinds of results that quickly. Like many others, he informed me that I was "full of it." I used my standard response: "Pick one person from your sales staff. I will work with that person and if you see the results, you can hire me. If there are no results, it won't cost you a cent." The next day he called me and gave me his employee's name.

I phoned her, we met, worked together, and then met again the following week for a follow-up. This woman made so many changes in one week that the president of the company called me in and asked how soon I could make a presentation for the rest of the sales staff. We set up a meeting and the result was 40 sales people and eight managers took part in the process. The company was good enough to let me keep track of all of the sales figures for 15 of the top sales people who had been involved. From the previous year, on average, they increased their individual sales by 65.8 per cent.

One of the top sales managers said: "Since I took your course, sales of my specific product have increased 176 per cent and profit has increased 244 per cent. As the self-proclaimed world's greatest skeptic, I fully endorse this course…"

This success was wonderful and helped me deal with my disappointment, now that it appeared the dream of a Wholeness Center was not going to happen – at least not on Prince Edward Island. I decided to concentrate on what was working and just let the rest of the dream unfold, as it was meant to, in its own good time. I had made the trip west on my own and now I felt Calgary had a promising future, so three months later Wilma and the children joined me.

The next company I worked with was a life insurance and financial planning company. Dwayne was a financial services representative when he was *asked* to meet me in August of 1997. Dwayne's work performance had slipped so dramatically that his boss Grant felt some outside assistance might be appropriate.

Dwayne had recently lost the person closest to him: his father died in a tragic car accident several months before. Dwayne and his father were very close, best friends. They played on the same hockey team, and took all sorts of weekend trips together. His death came just days before a special trip they had planned to take to the mountains. "We were going to ride horses just like we did when I was a kid. My life was very, very good up until that point."

After his Dad died, Dwayne recalls being completely lost. "I was in pretty rough shape, getting rougher all the time. I was a really good candidate for Donn to work with. I knew I wasn't doing well. It got so bad, I'd be at the elevator and know I had to go up – but to what floor? I'd just hang out there until someone I knew from my floor got in and I followed. I was miserable, but there was no way I'd ask for help." Dwayne was also frustrated because he had been a really creative thinker, full of concepts, ideas and innovative ways of handling his clients' business. This had earned him a solid reputation with management and clients. At this point in his life, however, he was drained of all creative energy.

"That first session I knew Dad's death was affecting me, but didn't understand why. And I certainly didn't know to what degree. Donn zeroed in on the issue right away, when he asked me some questions about my Dad. He focused directly on my loss and in the first session I experienced a total release of the grief from losing my Dad. In the second session he asked me to think of people that Dad had impacted, all the people I knew Dad had touched in some way. I discovered there was actually a piece of my Dad in each of them. That had such a strong healing effect. First, the realization of what was really bothering me and then to learn how to let go of the pain and loss.

"After my two sessions with Donn the administrative staff in the office asked what had happened; I had been so miserable and now I was so happy. They didn't know I was working with Donn as that was private between my boss Grant and me. There was a really noticeable change! I noticed it myself."

I knew in the business world how important it is to measure changes in concrete ways. I gave Dwayne a Stress Map Questionnaire from the Center for Higher Performance, before and after working with him. I had researched different tools and the one I finally chose measures the individual's level of stress in 21 areas of his life: work pressures, personal pressures, self-care, self-esteem, physical symptoms and more. Dwayne's responses are listed below.

Essi Systems Stress Map® Questionnaire: Test Results

STRESS LEVEL/PERFORMANCE (out of 21 variables)	BEFORE	AFTER 2ND SESSION	AFTER 3 MONTHS
Optimal	1	5	19
In Balance	3	15	2
Strain	5	1	0
Burnout	12	0	0

"The Essi System Inc," Canadian Corporate Edition published by the Center for High Performance, Collingwood, Ontario, Canada. The system was developed by Esther M. Orioli, M.S., Dennis T. Jaffe, Ph.D. and Cynthia D. Scott, Ph.D. M.P.H.

Before we worked together Dwayne was experiencing strain or burnout in 17 out of 21 variables. We only had two sessions, but I waited for three months before retesting to be sure the results were lasting. After that time Dwayne rated 19 areas in Optimal and 2 in Balance. What is interesting to me, in contrast with the common pattern, is that things continued to get better and better for Dwayne after the second session, with no other follow-up, while with many approaches the positive results wear off.

At the office Dwayne started closing business deals, opening new doors and taking the kinds of risks he never dreamed of doing in the past. He now manages the number-one Member CARE Financial Services office in Canada. As he puts it, "I just believed in myself, that I could do it." And there is more to the story than simply Dwayne's return to 'glory' in the office.

The most heart-warming feedback I got from Dwayne was when he said, publicly, "My 41 per cent gain is monetary, but that is only five per cent of what I truly got from the process. My whole life changed for the better including, nine months later, my wife having a baby." Dwayne and his family also realized another dream: they made the decision to move back to a small town in Saskatchewan, a move they had wanted to make for years.

Five years later Dwayne reports, "Part of what I did with Donn touches every part of my life today. He came into my life when things were very difficult for me and helped me get over them. Without him I don't think I would have recovered from my loss. Something else would have happened completely. I would have deteriorated until… who knows?"

In the corporate world I think it is often hard for people to get the support they need on issues like grief. I had another opportunity to help a client who was having trouble in business because of his distress. Richard works in financial planning as an executive consultant. He is an incredible person, one of the most intelligent guys I have ever met, and his wife was dying from cancer.

I remember when Richard invited me to meet his wife Gayle. She had already been through the traditional, invasive methods of Western medicine – radiation, chemotherapy and surgery – and was in the last stages of cancer. I wish I had the tools then that I have today; I have a deep sense that the process could have helped her more and the results could have been life changing.

Richard and Gayle had four daughters. The whole family was struggling with Gayle's illness and they were committed to not letting the illness tear the family apart. My focus initially was on Gayle. Richard reports: "Donn worked with Gayle and we enjoyed the tremendous benefits of her improved quality of life. Although the cancer was at a biological stage too advanced for treatment, by working with Donn, Gayle's emotional well-being was freed and her final journey was free of the emotional pain."

I also worked with Richard during this time and following Gayle's passing. "Donn was instrumental in assisting me through the grieving process and it has been a deeply rewarding journey. I am fortunate to be able to say I have grieved richly and well."

I took Richard through a process that assists people, who are grieving, in shifting their focus from loss to connection. They can still value and feel connected to everything a person stood for and embodied in their life. When people make this connection internally, it allows them to dwell on all that they gained from knowing and loving the person, rather than dwelling on their loss. When a ship sails out of the harbor and over the horizon, does it still exist? Yes, it does. I know you can stay connected to all of what you value in another person. Richard expresses it very eloquently:

"When people die there is a separation. We must make the journey to reconnect to everything that individual stood for. To take all their values, their gifts and internalize them, to keep them deep inside all the time, so there is no separation. It allows you to grieve in the most meaningful sense of the word."

The difference between Dwayne's case and Richard's was that Dwayne was resisting the grieving; he was suspended in time, not able to picture a future that didn't include his Dad. This strain showed up in every area of his life. Richard, on the other hand, allowed himself to grieve even during Gayle's illness. Before we worked together Dwayne was in complete denial about the impact his Dad's death was having on him. He wasn't aware of the strong sense of loss that was a cloud all around him. As soon as we began to explore this issue, he became acutely aware of his loss and how overwhelmed he felt with these feelings. This was why, in fact, he had suppressed them. Unfortunately, his total system was impacted by "depressing" these feelings. With help he was able to shift his focus from loss to the reserves he actually had deep within himself, and then his feelings shifted instantly. There is a profound difference between addressing an issue intellectually and having an experience that shifts the whole nervous system from constriction to openness. What I have said sounds simple when described like this, but many things can complicate the matter. For instance, many people who experience grief tap into earlier experiences of feeling like a victim. If this happens, the grief is compounded and all the previous experiences must be dealt with to release the constriction in the system.

Any kind of emotion that is not addressed, whether it is anger, resentment, loneliness, sadness or grief, suppresses the immune system and prevents the body from operating optimally. The damage can penetrate far deeper than what we might notice on the surface and can affect the person's entire physiology. The grieving process I offered Richard was the same process I used on myself as I watched my Dad deteriorate over five years before he died of Alzheimer's disease.

I found this time of my life very hard; as one of Dad's favourites I had a very close bond with him. I found out how bad his Alzheimer's was the day I went for a drive with Mom and Dad. Dad was driving and I watched Mom telling him when to stop for a light, when to change lanes and what speed to go. It was clear Dad wasn't fit to drive and I was afraid if his licence wasn't taken away, someone would be killed. So with the help of my two sisters we got the doctor to request a driver's test. Of course, Dad failed it and he was furious. Here was a man who drove professionally all his life. He blamed me for the loss of his licence and, true to form, he punished me by not speaking to me or my family for a whole year. For me this was a double loss, losing the connection with him due to the illness and being punished and isolated from the parent I was closest to.

Dr. David R. Hawkins addresses emotions like grief in his book *Power versus Force.** He outlines the energy fields of consciousness and identifies different levels of consciousness that correlate with emotions, perceptions, attitudes, world views and spiritual beliefs. Peace is calibrated at 600 on a scale of 1,000, courage is 200 and anger is 150. Grief has been calibrated as an energy level of 75. "This is the level of mourning, bereavement and remorse about the past. In grief, we see sadness everywhere. In grief, we confront the feeling that what has been lost, or the meaning it symbolizes, is irreplaceable."

I know many people believe that grieving has to take its natural course and you can't rush it. This may be a 'normal' view of grief, but it isn't necessarily true. From my experience and the experience of clients who I have helped deal with grief, grieving does not need to take years as traditionally thought. We can have a tremendous influence on the length of time we grieve by **how** we grieve. Time is not the crucial variable; it is the meaning we give to the loss and our ability or lack of ability to see beyond the loss. In some cultures death is viewed as a passing from one world to another and there is a great celebration, just as if a person was moving from one country to another. The joy and celebration is as instantaneous as the experience of grief.

* See bibliography

Our spirit is like a soaring eagle wanting to be free. Whenever it is constricted by strong emotions such as anger, panic or grief there is immense pain. We are meant to experience and release emotions quickly, not hold onto them for long periods of time. Hence when I work with people to release their grief there is a wonderful surge of expansive energy and a reawakening of the connection to their spirit. Many people experience this reawakening in their spirituality through the process. As one person expressed it to me, "…once the contamination was out of my system I was free for the first time in my life to have a spiritual relationship, built not on dependency and neediness, but on strength and wholeness."

This is not something I consider a goal or agenda; I don't impose beliefs on anyone. But there is a natural deepening that seems to happen. Because of my earlier experiences when I felt totally pure and free, I know that the core of every human being is also that pure and beautiful. When I am able to help someone strip away layers of contamination that mask who they are, they naturally find their true being. Richard comments on his spiritual journey, which began long before he met me. His work with me freed him to discover a whole new level of spirituality. As he expresses it, our ego, which I call the *developed ego*, limits us in so many ways.

"Life is completely, wholly, deeper, richer because I have been released from my stuck states. As a result I am experiencing a much richer spiritual journey. Spirituality to me is accepting that my ego isn't at the center of the universe and that I can find my way if I am listening. Relationships get richer when we listen deeper. If I have all my stress, my angst and denial with me, I am not listening. My ability to listen is directly related to my stuck or unstuck state."

So what is all this talk about stuck and unstuck? Richard has a great way of explaining it: "Have you ever walked into the mud and had your boots stick? As kids, we would stand there and holler for someone to help us, without even trying to pull our feet out. We'd just stay stuck. And to make matters worse – we'd blame someone else, when we were the ones who walked right into the mud."

Richard certainly knew about being stuck. He is extremely articulate, highly competent and very successful, but credits a lot of his success to his obsessive compulsiveness; his stressed-out, fast-paced existence. Even his own kids referred to him as "Mr. Hyper" or "Mr. Anal Retentive."

"My wife used to say that I wasn't able to relax unless the countertops were so clean you could eat off of them. I was really stuck. Now my kids see me as loose and laid back. It's a fabulous shift for me and for them. Stepping into that mud takes one step, stepping out takes another, but too many people are afraid to take that step. We end up stuck. It's like playing that same tape in our minds. I call it driving the BMW, Bitching Moaning and Whining. If you can't accept the responsibility for stepping into the mud in the first place, then you are stuck.

"I used to take everything so personally," adds Richard. "I understand now that a person can have issues that leave them stuck in a state of thinking, or reacting. If they unload anger at me that does not mean I'm responsible. Their anger is their emotion. They are fully responsible for themselves as I am. This has been a key insight in deepening and enriching relationships for me, at home and at work.

"Most therapy is like peeling an onion. You peel away a layer and there's a sense of accomplishment, but there is immediately another layer of onion to deal with. It shouldn't take 40 years, going back through every friggin' moment and issue you've been through in your life.

"I like Donn's paint analogy. Every experience, positive and negative, is a layer of paint, stroked onto your cabinet until one day you can't even see the detail work on the cabinet. Removing one layer at a time is a slow and painful process. But Donn has a gift; he can pinpoint the base layer and remove it. And what happens when we remove that very first layer of paint? The others automatically fall off! That is exactly what I experienced with Donn, in a few hours I had removed it all. It was exciting and exhausting. The impact of this work affected all areas of my life."

Richard and his family handled Gayle's death with courage and confidence, surpassing any process he thought was possible. She died in February and for the rest of that year, Richard spent only 39 days in the office. His primary focus was his family and supporting the girls through this tough time. During this period he made Top of the Round Table, which only half of one per cent of financial planners in the world attain, the elite of the elite. Richard said this happened effortlessly, when he went to work he was so clear and focused, everything just flowed.

Richard also encouraged all four girls to take the process. The opportunity to help Richard and his family find the extraordinary within them was a wonderful, rewarding journey. Helping one person transform their life is very rewarding, but even more rewarding is seeing a family come closer together, handling adversity with courage and ultimately flourishing. Every community, province or country is made up of families, and reaching these families is what builds the foundation for a world that is rich and rewarding for all of us.

REFINING, STREAMLINING, FLYING HIGHER

8

One's destination is never a place,
but rather a new way of looking at things.
HENRY MILLER, 1891 – 1980

THE RESULTS WITH RICHARD AND HIS FAMILY WERE GRATIFYING, but I recognized I was still measuring my own value and self-worth by the results my clients achieved. I knew this was serious. When clients either didn't get the results or minimized the results, I felt powerless and I pushed even harder to find answers. I always wanted to go faster. Speed was exciting, whether it was driving a car or working with a client.

But speed wasn't the real issue. The real issue was tied to my self-esteem and my coping pattern of self-reliance. I still felt I was "on my own" and it was up to me to make it all happen. The more I could accomplish, the better I felt about myself and the happier I was. The faster I went, the more I could get done in a day, a month or a year. Not only did I want to go faster, I wanted to fly higher and move further ahead. Whatever hadn't been accomplished I was drawn to, like a moth to a light. But I was still dodging the core issue.

I knew there was one area where speed was a real asset – in the world of sports. One of my passions was working with athletes and for them, the faster and more effectively they can perform, the more successful they are. I wanted to focus on very specific aspects of performance; namely, how athletes reach their highest level of performance and what stops them from playing at that level with consistency. In choosing to focus on sports, it seemed fitting to change the name of my process to align it with the new emphasis. This was the beginning of Zone State Conditioning, another significant milestone in my development.

In contrast to the Metamorphosis Model, Zone State Conditioning stressed performance and the elements that make up optimal performance. According to my way of thinking, the secret to optimal performance was locked in how an athlete handles a slump. **The slump holds the key to what needs to change.** It is like finding the combination to a safe. The limiting beliefs that an athlete has are always reflected in how he is thinking when he is in a slump. So, by closely examining the slump, I knew what to go after. This sounds simple, but in fact it took years to hone the skills to find the right combination for each athlete, quickly and with consistency. Once I developed this competency, the only variable that influenced the consistency of results was the athlete's degree of willingness to work with me.

NHL hockey players were just the type of athlete I wanted to work with. I already loved hockey, and whenever I saw a team that was not living up to its potential on a consistent basis, I wanted to jump in and assist. I love excellence; whether it is in a person or a team, I feel inspired by it. I believe our world is a better place whenever someone shows some form of excellence, in performance or in personal character. We all need examples of excellence. When that excellence is hampered I am immediately curious about why and what is needed to re-establish it. I know if excellence has been achieved even once, it can be repeated and maintained. Once the constrictions are dissolved the excellence is maintained with *effortless effort*.

I sent a promotional package to an NHL team and they replied within a week. With only 11 games left in the season, they were in danger of not making the playoffs. I met with the director of player personnel and, as before, he didn't believe an athlete could achieve the results I claimed – and definitely not in the short time I predicted. But he agreed to talk to the general manager. The next morning the GM called me himself, and after discussing the process at length, he identified two players he felt needed some outside help.

A few minutes later he called to tell me one of the players was interested – but the other didn't want anything to do with it because he thought it was the traditional sports psychology 'stuff.' The GM wanted to know how long it would take to get the interested player back on his game. The player had been off for three months with an injury. He'd worked very hard to get his body back in shape and once he returned, he thought everything would be fine. He was wrong! After about 20 games he had lost his confidence and couldn't seem to regain it. He was one of their best players, but he definitely was not showing that on the ice.

I said: It will take approximately five hours. The GM didn't believe me. "No, no, Mr. Smith, you must have heard me wrong; he has been off his game all year and now he's got no confidence whatsoever. I want to know how long you think it's going to take to get this player on top of his game."

I replied: Well sir, I know you don't have any experience with what I have to offer, but if the player's willing, it will take about five hours. With great doubt in his voice he said, "OK, he's got a game at seven tonight, can you be here at three today?" I knew this was his way of challenging me, of saying: Put your money where your mouth is – and that was fine with me, because I knew in my heart what was possible.

Earlier, when we talked about fees, I was so confident in the work the player and I could do together and the results we could get, I offered a contract that charged 10 per cent of my fee upfront and 90 per cent if the team made it into the playoffs.

Working with a player at three in the afternoon on game day is unheard of. In normal circumstances it would never happen because a player is so focused on his game that he'd never take time out to try anything different, especially something he'd never heard of. And most players would never attempt to integrate something new into their system that close to game time. From a traditional perspective, both the player and the general manager were taking an incredible risk and I appreciated that.

I met the player at three; he didn't know me from Adam, didn't know what I did. But he did know how deep an emotional pit he had dug himself into and he was open to anything. We spent an hour-and-a-half together and after the game I asked him how he felt. He told me: "For the first two periods I was able to hold onto everything we'd worked on, but in the last period I felt as if I'd run out of gas." He wanted to know what we could do to finish the process and he wanted to do it ASAP. "Can we meet before practice tomorrow morning?" he asked. We met for two more hours and after that session he was back on top of his game. Three more short sessions, totaling 30 minutes, kept him at the top of his game for the rest of the regular season and playoffs. Yes, they did make it to the playoffs!

Remember how skeptical the general manager was? In the paper the morning after our first session, he was quoted as saying it was the best game that player had played all season. His teammates could see the changes, too. And the player who said he didn't want to have anything to do with this stuff came up to me the next day and said, "I don't know what you did with my buddy, but I want the same."

The high of working with players and seeing the tremendous gains they were able to make overnight was wonderful. The results were so tangible and measurable. This was a great change from working with emotional issues that can be elusive when measuring effectiveness. In the world of performance every second can count and this immediacy demands a process that is streamlined and produces results. This fast-paced world was exhilarating, but there was a downside I wasn't expecting. Dealing with the complex dynamics involved in such a high-profile sport as hockey was something I was totally unprepared for. I was no longer just working with a player and getting individual results; there were many other factors to contend with in the world of professional sport. Issues like strong egos, politics, control of power, to mention just a few.

High-performance athletes, just like anyone else, can have limiting beliefs. Robert Dilts, a very creative trainer in the NLP community, calls these *thought viruses*. He describes how a virus can sit dormant inside a computer until a certain cue triggers it. Once triggered, the virus can interfere with the full use of data and software in the system. Low self-esteem can be viewed as a thought virus. As soon as it's in our system it creates havoc. Beliefs like "slumps are normal" open the door to accepting slumps or injuries as something you cannot control. I believe whatever you think will happen is going to happen; I know this from personal experience. As soon as I started to think I was inadequate as a goalie, it was all downhill for me. My hot and cold track record was a result of letting one goal through, and thinking I was a failure. This hot and cold pattern didn't just happen in hockey. It followed me into baseball, too, because the thought virus was inside of me, not in the sport.

THOUGHT VIRUSES

Thought viruses are beliefs that limit us in our ability to be healthy, enjoy well-being and perform at our best. All limiting beliefs are like computer viruses. When they are activated, we constrict our energy and lose access to our skills and resourcefulness. The beliefs lie dormant in our minds waiting to be activated. When they are triggered, we experience a constriction of our energy, and our performance, well-being and health suffer.

Personally I also came to a sobering realization from working with elite performers: even though the results were great, and my process was much more streamlined, it still needed refinement. I wanted to refine my process so it worked with greater speed and precision. Part of the honing came through doing more work with major health issues. My interest in health paralleled my interest in sports; the challenge of both fascinated me. While I was working with the NHL team, I was also working with a woman named Chris who suffered from chronic fatigue and fibromyalgia. The severity of Chris's fibromyalgia had been medically classified at 9.5 on a 10-point scale, meaning she had very extensive impairment. Not only were 18 points diagnosed throughout her body, she had also lost 85 per cent of her muscle strength and most of her glands, joints and lymph nodes had swelled and hardened. She was tired and in pain all the time, she needed help to bathe, dress and write. Her energy was so low she had not been able to work in five years.

The shift she made was dramatic and rapid. After the first two sessions she went from resting several times a day to ease the pain, to 14-hour days of pain-free time and much more energy. Her chronic conditions of irritable bowel syndrome and diverticulosis diminished significantly and she no longer required extensive diet restrictions. Ten weeks later she was back working full-time, enjoying a busy social life, renewed spirituality and feeling full of energy. She said her thinking had changed; it was so clear and quick now, it was almost mind-boggling.

Six months later Chris sent me a follow-up letter. She said her future had never looked so bright. Physically, even when she does overdo it, the pain doesn't return. She just gets a tingling sensation that lets her know her body is tired. What a remarkable change!

Having gotten the results she wanted, Chris decided she would come with me to a Health Expo in Calgary, to share her experiences with others. I too was pleased and excited with the results that Chris attained and thought we would have a great time sharing this success at the Expo. We were like kids at the candy store thinking everybody at the Expo would be interested in what we had to say. To my complete and utter amazement this is not what happened. For one reason or another, people wanted to discount our experience.

Chris wanted people to know there was an alternative to chronic pain.

We both thought our listeners would share our excitement, but instead they were deeply skeptical. Even when Chris talked about her specific results, they remained unconvinced. She was shocked by this and I was frustrated. I just didn't understand this way of thinking, when it came to health. The thought viruses were definitely more pervasive than I had realized. I saw people practically dying from one illness or another, who were still closed to new ideas. The fears preventing them from being open to anything new – fear of the unknown, fear of change, fear of losing control – were the same fears that were creating the constrictions in their bodies and showing up in disease of one form or another. And speaking of patterns, here was my pattern again: I got my hopes up and was all excited about what could happen at the Expo and then down I went, feeling hopeless and full of despair. Would things ever change? Would people ever be interested in what I had to offer?

But one young man, Kevin, had the opposite reaction. His attitude was, "Show me, man: if you can do what you say you can do, I'm in." Kevin was certainly in bad shape when we met. But, even with all the negative thinking he describes in his letter below, he was highly motivated to change. Part of why I love working with young men and women is to help them avoid some of the pain and suffering I experienced. Here is Kevin's story:

"I am a 19-year-old college student who has always been a negative person. In May of 1997 that negative thinking came to a head; I experienced high stress, high anxiety, almost total sleeplessness, violent thoughts, heavy depression, accompanied by heavy drinking. At this point I turned to the medical profession for help. They made me fill out a bunch of forms, and then prescribed some pills that would take at least a month to start working. Things were getting worse by the moment and I was losing hope. When I heard of Donn Smith, I turned to him as a last resort. Meeting Donn, I had no expectations or preconceived notions of what he did. After two sessions, a total of six hours, I had a complete change in thinking. Not only

did I return to my original state of mind, but I gained tools that would lead to my ultimate success and happiness. To this day, the changes are still in place and growing. I truly believe he saved my life."

In my work I never focus on symptoms. If I had, Kevin and I would have been working together for 20 years. Instead, I work on what causes the symptoms. There's an old story I like to tell about a water-damaged ceiling tile: replacing the ceiling tile is useless until you fix the leak that caused the damage in the first place. Whether we are talking about ceiling tiles or human beings we still need to solve problems, not put bandaids over them. Sherry is a wonderful example of a lady who had done lots of work on symptoms but was still struggling. She hadn't dealt with the real cause of her problem.

I first met Sherry in the fall of 1999, while she was researching a documentary for CBC television on using humor to treat depression. She had heard about "this guy who does this profound shift on a deep level" from Wendy, a woman who had experienced the process. Since Sherry had a history of mania and depression, often called Bipolar Personality Disorder, and had already tried a number of approaches, she was more than curious about my work. We arranged to meet and here is Sherry's first impression:

"Donn walked into Earl's Restaurant looking every inch the Calgary executive. But the suit was merely window dressing. Warm. That is the first thought that comes to mind when you meet Donn. You know how some people do that limp-wrist, wet-fish handshake? Well, Donn's is one I will never forget. Strong, warm and I swear, tingling. When he greets you he looks you square in the eyes. He holds your gaze for that second longer than you are used to. It is a gaze I soon discovered is hard to avoid.

"We talked for a while, then he turned and asked me directly: Do you want to keep your manic depressive patterns forever? I was taken aback. No, I sputtered, I don't. He continued: There is a high probability this process can help you. Egged on by a glass of Sauvignon Blanc I said: Oh hell, let's do it. I was so petrified by what Donn was suggesting – I knew if I didn't say yes right then, I'd find excuses until the cows came home."

Sherry goes on to describe her first session:

"The minute Donn began asking me questions I knew this was going to be different from every other therapy session I had ever had. Donn is like that annoying five-year-old who refuses to accept your answers. Why? he asks. When I say: because I am always angry, he doesn't let up. Now I must say right here he is not demeaning or belittling or aggressive in his questioning. He is simply inquisitive and his inquisitiveness forces you to look beyond the answers you have blindly given yourself over the years. Suddenly you are giving yourself a whack upside the head and thinking: Oh my God – how come that never occurred to me before?

"Then the real work begins. He is gentle, reassuring and calming as you work neurologically on your life experiences. Just through questions I was able to identify the real issues I needed to address and to release the emotions that kept me stuck. **One of the things that fascinated me was how Donn would connect physical pain to emotional issues.** I had recently seen a specialist and was facing exploratory surgery on my left knee. When I told Donn this, he asked me what I was afraid of moving forward on?

"Huh? Well the surgery…

"No, Sherry – think beyond that. Knee pain is symbolic of the fear of moving forward with your life – what are the steps you want to take in your life that you're afraid to step into?

"I thought about it for awhile and then I gave him my answers. My fears of the future immobilized me in the present.

"It was the most intense five hours of my life. But I never felt compromised or awkward. I just felt enormous relief that I was finally being called on everything I have always thought about myself. It was like the mirror in Snow White, telling me to see it like it really was. I walked away that day with the most profound sense of self-love I have ever experienced. I made two new friends that day: Donn and this absolutely charming and life-loving woman named Sherry.

"I also had this transforming experience when I came home after that very first session with Donn. When I saw Scott, my husband, I was startled. I felt as though I was looking at him for the very first time, finally seeing him. His eyes were unbelievably beautiful. I felt myself gasp for air. I saw so far inside his eyes it made me realize that, all this time, here was this man who had stood beside me through so much of my inner turmoil and who had suffered first-hand my insecure lashings and withdrawals. I felt his energy and for the first time in my life realized this guy is my soul-mate."

THE MIND BODY CONNECTION

9

To first understand the bodymind connection
we first have to recognise that the mind and body are one.
DEBBIE SHAPIRO

SHERRY'S COMMENT ABOUT THE CONNECTION BETWEEN THE body and the mind is pivotal to the work I do. This connection is so fundamental that whenever a client has a physical injury or illness, I automatically look for the emotional connection. The body actually mirrors what is going on emotionally within us. This may seem hard to believe, but if you think in terms of energy and constriction, wherever energy is constricted there will be distress. Each part of the body is designed to perform certain functions. In Sherry's case her knee was showing the distress. Legs are designed to carry us forward and the knees are there for flexibility, so I naturally wondered what she was afraid to move forward on. Cyril is another great example of what I am talking about.

Cyril was facing serious challenges in his life and they were affecting his health in a big way. I met him at a convention for life insurance agents where I was the guest speaker. He came up to me after the presentation and said he wanted to meet with me as soon as he could, to work on his performance. Many clients initially seek help for a particular issue, but that's only a small part of what needs to be addressed. Cyril was focusing on motivation and performance, which for me are symptoms, and I am interested in the cause. Cyril was also suffering serious pain in his hip, shoulder and knee from arthritis, as a result of old sports injuries. He had played rugby, football, and had done a lot of steer wrestling. In addition to his physical distress, Cyril's wife was dying of cancer. All in all, plenty of reason for distress, but just because stress makes "sense" doesn't mean it is inevitable. We have a great deal of influence over what our systems do.

As I started asking Cyril questions about what motivated him to see me, I noticed he was physically wincing. I asked him why he was so uncomfortable and Cyril explained the serious injuries to his hip, shoulder and knee. "I am scheduled for knee and shoulder surgery immediately and my hip needs replacing in the next two years." I suggested to Cyril there might be a way to deal with the pain. Cyril was skeptical, but he said, "When you're in pain you'll reach for anything. You have to give everything a shot." For me to help Cyril, he needed to understand the connection between the mind and the body, so I told him about my back problems.

In 1974 I stepped off a curb approximately three feet high and, all of a sudden, my lower back was in excruciating pain. This back pain continued intermittently for 12 years, during which time I went to chiropractors, doctors and physiotherapists. I tried everything. The specialists were telling me I had deformed disks in my lower back that possibly needed surgery. My back consistently went out three or four times a year.

One time I remember being in bed for eight days; physically, I could not move. The pain was so bad I started crying. I was home by myself, lying really still, trying not to move and crying in pain. Once again I had a sense of powerlessness. I hated waiting for my back to go out, not knowing when I would be plunged into pain, and believing I had no control over changing it other than with pain killers and muscle relaxants. For 12 years I thought the problem was my back, but it wasn't.

At that time I didn't know there was any connection between how I was thinking, perceiving myself and my world, and my lower back. I didn't know my lower back problems came from the insecurity I felt, my fear of dealing with the world. Basically, I had such a need to control things that my back just got tighter and tighter – it got so tight that something had to give. Then I would be flat on my back, my body would release the tension and I would be OK for another three months.

This cycle continued until 1984 when I said to myself, this is bullshit, the back is not the problem! I started reviewing the past and realized that each time my back went out, there was a buildup of unpleasant emotions, mostly anger. My job wasn't solid, there were financial difficulties and I felt very insecure. Every three or four months this pressure escalated to a point where my 'back' went out.

Debbie Shapiro, in her book *The Bodymind Workbook**, explores the relationship between the body and the mind. She links the type of back problem I was having with insecurities around finances. That fit me perfectly. Once I realized this, I addressed my issues of insecurity and that was it. The back problem disappeared. No one has ever treated my back and I have not had a twinge since 1984.

I now know that if I had been in a relaxed, humorous, playful state, I could have stepped off a curb twice as high and been fine. When you're in the flow and in harmony with the universe, it's a bounce – not a break. Change is not sudden or jarring to the system. You are in the flow. That's why an athlete can be checked into the boards 2,000 times with no injury. Then, one night something's going on – he's had a big fight with his wife, he's in contract negotiations or having trouble with a teammate or he hasn't been scoring goals. That's when something's liable to break. And what will break is the part of the body related to the psychological issue. But if he is in the zone, he'll have the fluidity that's like a large beach ball bouncing to the

* See bibliography

ground; it just bounces back.

So I really understood where Cyril was coming from and I knew I could help him if he was willing. At one point in the session Cyril confessed his pain from the arthritis was so unbearable, he had been thinking: "I have to get off this earth because I can't stand the pain."

I still remember his enthusiasm when this 6'3", 220 lb. man came back 10 days later with *no pain at all* in any of his joints. In Cyril's own words, after the second session, "Since doing the process I've had no pain in my shoulder, no pain in my knee and no hip pain." Four years later Cyril proudly reports, "I was at the specialist a couple of months ago and he said the hip they recommended replacing was now OK, structurally. It still has arthritis, but they have changed their minds about a replacement and the shoulder and the knee have regenerated." What shocked Cyril the most was the speed with which the changes occurred.

Cyril's reaction reflects a very common thought virus: *change takes time*. I hear this from all kinds of people: athletes, performers, businessmen. But I knew change could happen quickly. I was always looking for ways to speed up the change process – not to make it go faster than normal – just to go at the rate that change occurs naturally in the body. Remember when I talked about phobias people develop early in life? Most people who have a phobia only need one experience to lock the fear into their nervous system. I knew if they could lock a phobia into their system in seconds, they could unlock it almost as quickly, if someone showed them how. The rate of change is also tied to the ability to get to the constriction in a person's body at the cellular level, not the intellect. To understand the differences in making changes at the levels of the intellect, the nervous system and the cellular level I'd like to use the computer as an illustration. Making changes at the intellectual level is like making changes in the document you are working on. Changes at the nervous system level are like getting a new computer program and changes at the cellular level are like rewriting the hard drive.

Dr. Bruce Lipton, a cellular biologist at Stanford University, has drawn fascinating conclusions from his study of cells, with promising implications for the link between perception, cellular growth and the body's ability to regenerate at a cellular level. He views the 50 to 70 trillion cells in a person's body as mini-computers responding to messages from the environment – both the external and internal environments.

When chemical signals are received from the external environment, they lead the cell to generate an appropriate response. The person's **interpretations** of the environment as safe or threatening, based on beliefs developed in childhood, become internal signals that lead cells to generate the response. These signals Dr. Lipton refers to are the mechanisms I **knew** were in people's systems. They are the triggers that need to be identified and dissolved in order to have the system geared for growth. If we don't dissolve these triggers, what we scan for on our internal radar screen is whether or not we are safe; this leaves our system tense and constantly on guard.

If we perceive safety or love, cells enter growth mode. This means they stay healthy because in life, if an organism is not growing, it's dying. Energy is available for living and learning and growing. In response to an environment we perceive as threatening, cells enter their protective mode: that means all growth shuts down. Our bodies are not meant to remain tense in protective mode for extended periods of time. When we have a belief that leads to continual interpretations of danger or threat, our cells, or at least a portion of them, stop growing. Over time stress symptoms may appear.

Conflicting beliefs within a person – like "I must succeed" and "I'm worthless" – are more confusing because they are contradictory and so some of our cells obey one belief and other cells obey the opposing belief. This creates internal conflict and again some form of physical distress may appear if it continues over a period of time. At first, the symptoms may simply be a decrease in energy and difficulty mobilizing a full-strength response to whatever is happening. But, as the protective response continues, disease symptoms become more likely.

Many highly successful people seem to function well, in spite of limiting or constricting beliefs, many of which can be unconscious. Although they don't let the limiting beliefs stop them from moving forward, they do pay a price. Constricting beliefs always use up energy and interfere with the body and mind functioning as well as they could. Imagine how much more a person is capable of when all internal messages enhance growth responses and high energy levels, rather than fear-based protective responses.

Dr. Lipton's research was confirming everything I believed and it was exciting to have the scientific data to support what I had personally been seeing in my work with clients. When I think back to my earlier experiences of feeling pure, whole and completely at peace, there is no doubt my whole being – cells included – was wide open and free flowing. This was my goal for everyone I worked with, clearing out any triggers that would tell the cells to constrict. I knew humans could attain this state of peace and joy while being fully engaged in life. Although I still didn't have all the pieces, I was a lot closer; the process was definitely more powerful and I was taking on bigger and bigger challenges.

When I met Kathy she was at a very difficult point in her life. She was facing brain surgery in eight days to have a tumor removed. The tumor had been diagnosed in March 2001. By the time she saw me in August of that year, she had built up an overwhelming fear of the surgery. The tumor was affecting her eyesight and, without treatment, she would eventually go blind in both eyes. "I was pretty freaked out, my vision was quite bad in one eye and getting worse, and I was terrified about the surgery."

I vividly recall how terrible Kathy looked the day we met and yet two sessions later she was so peaceful. This was just two days before the operation. She and I had worked on connecting with that inner place of peace far removed from where Kathy had been focusing.

Kathy admits to being a fear junkie. "I was comfortable being afraid." She was very competitive and sought out sports that pushed her adrenaline. At work, she operated on a fear basis, taking on too many projects at once, facing looming deadlines. In her 20s she became an alcoholic and drug addict. Kathy sought help for her addictions and hadn't touched a drink in 23 years. But the fear was still there in her system.

"When I went through the process I felt completely freed. Things that were difficult and insurmountable didn't even seem to be an issue. I had a real change, a 180-degree turn, in how I looked at the world and my relationships with people."

Kathy discovered she didn't have to make things really difficult in order to make her success that much greater. "All my life I would set things up to be really, really difficult and then, against all odds, I would succeed. I found I didn't have to do that anymore. I didn't have to make it so hard all the time. Or work under so much fear. Removing that kind of fear and pressure lightened my load. I just felt better about myself."

Whatever the person perceives as most valuable is what our innate instincts will use to get our attention. As Kathy says, "All my life I've valued my brain and my intelligence and it was very difficult to accept that someone was going to operate on my brain." It may seem ironic or just plain unfair that the thing a person values most is taken away from them, but there is method in this madness. I remember meeting a lady with MS and the thing she missed most was playing the piano. If our innate spirit is trying to get our attention, it makes sense it will focus on something we care deeply about.

The tumor operation was scheduled for mid-October. "By the time of the surgery my attitude had turned around, my constrictions just let go; I was going to have the surgery and I knew it was going to be OK."

Kathy became a miracle patient. "I came through the anaesthetic with no problems, despite my blood pressure and weight. I was out of the hospital in three-and-a-half days. In two weeks I was back to normal. It was my new positive attitude. The doctor was astounded at my recovery and how I came through the operation. Six months later my vision was completely normal.

"I feel great. I'm in much better physical shape now. I find it's easier to care for myself. My attitude changed: instead of thinking I'm being deprived, I'm looking after myself better. I'm really enjoying working out. I do weights and I just love it. I've lost weight, I'm much more supple and flexible and I am back playing golf, something I missed immensely."

The real test came when Kathy decided to build a new home. Doing this as a single mom, she discovered more new strength. "I had to make the bulk of the decisions. I found my stamina, my energy – everything was so much better than it would have been in the past. Before, I would have been so stressed, it would have been very difficult for everyone around me. Then I'd feel all alone, thinking I had to do all this myself. All that has shifted."

Kathy describes perfectly how destructive the self-reliance pattern can be in relationships, pushing people away under a guise of independence and then feeling abandoned when people naturally withdraw. Our behavior produces exactly the opposite of what we want. We want to be connected to people and yet when there is fear, our system naturally goes into protective mode and the barriers go up. Shifting this pattern was essential for Kathy to be truly happy.

For Kathy another problem area she had been refusing to address was relationships. After the process she was very clear what was the right direction for her to take. "I came to terms with a destructive relationship. I just had to let go of it. Looking back, I got very little out of it. I'm not interested in working at a relationship if it's at my expense." Kathy's interactions with her children also changed for the better, especially with her 19-year-old daughter Jacqueline.

I have discovered many people spend a great deal of time trying to control people, places and things outside of themselves and for the most part, to little avail. When Kathy changed what was going on internally, her relationships reflected this change. We have no control of people around us, despite how much we think we do or wish we did. But we can influence others, both positively and negatively.

I know the way I behaved – drinking, being angry and afraid – affected my children and my wife. Part of my search to change myself and, ultimately, help others was to make amends for how I influenced my loved ones. I have had the joy of assisting both my daughter and my son in releasing old hurts and reclaiming the beautiful person inside. The best influence we can have is to be true to who we really are.

When people are ready to make changes, it is easy to work with them. Readiness, I now recognize, is a vital factor. If a person isn't ready, it doesn't matter what skills I have. I remember working with a fellow from AA. One night Mike said he wanted to quit smoking. I had been quite successful helping people with that addiction, so we set an appointment. I spent three hours with Mike, doing everything I knew that had worked in the past. About 10 days later I saw Mike and asked him how he was doing. He said, "You know, Donn, it took me about four days before I could smoke again and not feel sick to my stomach." So the moral of the story is people can say they want to change, but it doesn't always mean they are ready to change.

What scares many people away from taking a big step towards change is their beliefs about what it is going to be like, based on what they have seen, heard or experienced. They expect it to be completely overwhelming, pain-filled and demoralizing. Imagine you are in a dark corner, feeling trapped and scared. From that perspective it seems almost impossible to imagine that you could just walk away from the corner and yet, psychologically, once the constriction is released, it can be just that simple.

Colleen, on the other hand, was a person who really wanted to change. In fact, she wanted to change most of her life but didn't know how. She had hit rock bottom. "I had been off work for about eight weeks from sheer physical exhaustion. I was experiencing chronic fatigue 24 hours a day, along with being depressed and having a lot of anger inside of me. I was not living life, I was simply existing."

Colleen couldn't walk more than two blocks without resting. She was too tired for friends and she was thinking constantly about her deceased mother. She began to wish she could join her mother, who had been gone for 20 years. She had just finished reading the book *Love, Medicine & Miracles**

* See bibliography

115

by Bernie S. Siegel and she started to cry as she realized what she was doing: slowly killing herself by shutting down her body. Colleen was shocked when I accurately assessed her state. "Donn knew. He said I was committing suicide in a way that would be socially acceptable. I couldn't believe he knew. That was when I knew Donn could help me and that I would do whatever it took to heal."

Colleen needed to address many emotional issues underpinning her chronic fatigue and fibromyalgia including 20 years of grief surrounding the loss of her mother. When we dealt with the underlying issues, she experienced a big release: "A peace came over me." Her thoughts changed dramatically and she was able to understand her past in a totally new way.

Interestingly enough, the first day I saw Colleen she was suffering another bout of strep throat. When the session ended her strep throat was gone. How could a chronic viral infection that has to be treated with weeks of antibiotics be gone in three hours, without any medical intervention? The answer is our system has incredible power to heal if we identify what is short-circuiting the system, just like an electrical system in our home. If we correct the short-circuit so we return to full power to heal, regenerate and flourish, the results can be as immediate as what Colleen experienced. As we addressed the unresolved emotional issues in Colleen's life the chronic fatigue and fibromyalgia quickly dissolved.

Below Colleen has charted the differences:

April 2000	April 2001
Sleeping all the time	Sleeping 6 to 7 hours a night with no naps during the day
No energy	Lots of energy; on the go 12 hours a day
Couldn't walk 2 blocks without resting	Walking 2-3 miles a day Riding my bike to work and back, while working 8.25 hours.
Constant yeast infections Heart palpitations Couldn't breathe Upset stomach	No longer experiencing heart palpitations, upset stomach, yeast infections, breathlessness
Lots of anger Depressed	Anger & depression have disappeared
Too tired to go out with friends	Looking forward to getting together with friends
Didn't want to live Slowly committing suicide by shutting down my body	I want to live & I look forward to the future
Felt like I had to be perfect Wanted to have control of everything	I no longer have the need to be perfect & control situations

"I'm so proud of myself because I've come a long way. I'm happy and full of energy. Just recently, I bought a new condo. I've wanted to do this for two years, but with my fatigue and depression, I just couldn't handle it." Colleen's closing line was: "I would like to thank you from the bottom of my heart and I will never forget you as long as I live, which will be a very, very long time."

10

Reality is merely an illusion, albeit a very persistent one.

ALBERT EINSTEIN, 1879 – 1955

SPEAKING OF SHOWING PEOPLE HOW TO HELP THEMSELVES, it was my turn to learn some new lessons again. My goal was still to assist people as much as I could, as quickly as possible, and have them run their own lives. I was so committed to this that on many occasions people said to me, "Donn, you are going to put yourself right out of work!" As unlikely as this sounds, wouldn't it be wonderful!

I was still refining my process, and in my never-ending search, I encountered *The Body Talk System** by Dr. John Veltheim. He was the first person I ever met who was getting similar results as quickly as I did, only in a totally different way. I was so intrigued I wanted to understand how his process worked. The training was so new that I became the second person in Canada to be certified.

* See bibliography

BODYTALK

> **BodyTalk** is a simple and effective form of therapy that allows the body's energy systems to be resynchronized so that it can operate as nature intended. Our energy systems become out of balance primarily through exposure to the stresses of day-to-day life. Resynchronizing them enables the body's mechanisms to function at optimal levels thus preventing disease and rapidly accelerating the healing process.

I learned a lot, but the most significant concept I learned was not from Body Talk training, but from John himself. He challenged me to recognize the difference between **knowing** and **believing**. I remember clearly the meeting in which I confronted John and took up 75 per cent of the time debating the issue. For me to accept what he had to say meant I had to let go of everything I believed to be true. I felt the ground shifting under me and I felt fear and panic: if this changes, what do I have to hold onto?

To understand the impact of this shift is likely difficult, but let me use gravity as a way of explaining how things changed for me. With gravity everything, including people, stays in place, held there by an invisible force. But when gravity is gone everything changes. Solid objects start floating around, including people, and nothing is the same. That's how I felt when John started to question my thinking around beliefs.

My work, I realized, was focused on beliefs – not on the knowing. I had been identifying positive and negative beliefs and helping people change the negative beliefs into positive ones. I didn't realize that beliefs about our identity, although significant, are still just beliefs – they are not the core of who we are. There is something deeper. I thought if you believed something, it was in essence a "fact." I was wrong.

Take a minute and ask yourself: If you really know something, does that feel different from believing something? Remember how I thought that I was stupid and for a long time nothing I did seemed to change that belief? Then, after taking courses and starting to enjoy learning, I began to believe

I wasn't stupid – I was smart. What I did was change my belief. Unfortunately, that only lasted until I met someone I thought was much smarter than me and, by comparison, I felt stupid all over again. Round and round this went, thinking I was stupid, trying to prove I wasn't, and subconsciously waiting for the next test – the next comparison – to see if I was indeed smart. Now I understood why I couldn't maintain my belief that I was smart. Many times, I changed my belief from "I am stupid, to I am smart," but underneath, the layer of doubt was still intact. There is a deeper level of "knowing" and once we connect with that core, the changes are permanent. Today I know there is *genius* in all of us and I have a deep knowing of the genius in me. It is not about comparisons with anyone else, the knowing is within me and unshakeable.

This was a pivotal turning point for me, acknowledging the difference between believing and knowing. The integration of this profound truth began shortly after I got over the shock that what I was presently doing was really only window dressing. I definitely needed to go deeper. Most people, including me, build their sense of well-being on their beliefs about themselves and the world. We use our accomplishments and our relationships as gauges for how well we are doing. That was why I was so driven to succeed. The idea that knowing is completely different from believing was profound. It was then that I realized the route I was taking to find and maintain inner peace was not going to work, at least not for the long term.

I knew I had to shift gears immediately. I was not settling for anything that was only going to last a short while. I was dedicated to finding a true, inner sustained peace that is completely natural. I knew this peace was not going to come from accomplishments, but rather from knowing, profoundly, who I truly am. Remember my earlier experiences – my first confession, my profound emotional release when I completed the fifth step in AA? Both experiences connected me to the very essence of my being and grounded within me a true sense of what *knowing* felt like. At the time, I didn't know these were pivotal experiences that would guide me like beacons of light towards a destination of long-lasting inner peace.

Inside of me I had a blueprint to follow, but I still had to figure out how to read it. I had tasted, first hand, the *knowing*. Now it was just a matter of how to go to that place consciously and consistently. Once there, it should be possible to lock in the *state of knowing* and rewire the nervous system to operate along these pathways, instead of the familiar constricted ones. I knew some people thought I was just another fool looking for the pot of gold at the end of the rainbow. Maybe I just wasn't willing to face reality, our humanness. Or maybe I just wanted an easy way out, a magic answer that would give me that lasting peace I craved. It was easy to go down this path on days when nothing seemed to work and yet, deep inside, a voice kept saying, No... there is a way and you are on the right track. This is important! Shifting from believing to knowing is the key. The voice was literally screaming at me to pay attention.

To illustrate my shift from beliefs to knowing, consider this metaphor – icicles. Icicles build up drop by drop, layer by layer, clinging tenaciously to roofs or drainpipes. Sometimes, they can be gleaming and beautiful and other times murky, cloudy and dirty. When the icicle is beautiful, clear and appealing, I compare it to positive beliefs. An icicle that is contaminated with dirt, roof debris or muddy water resembles our limiting beliefs. The key about both the clear and contaminated icicle is this: neither one is part of the building's structure. No matter what they look like, they will melt before July comes around. It is an illusion to think the icicle will last. Thinking we are a success or a failure, lovable or unlovable, is linking our identity to our beliefs, which is building identity on an illusion.

Another way to demonstrate the shift from beliefs to knowing is to use affirmations as an example. Today, for me, making affirmations is the same as looking in a mirror and saying I have a nose, I have a mouth, I have eyes. We don't do this because we **know** we have a mouth or eyes; so if we really know something, we don't make affirmations. And if we look in the mirror and say something we know to be false, such as "I have three eyes," it only registers disbelief.

When we make affirmations, we are trying to engrave in our minds, hearts and spirits things we **want** to be true. We are focusing on ideas we believe to be true while primarily engaging our minds. But thinking is very different from feeling, and believing something is profoundly different from knowing it heart and soul.

Many great teachers have offered affirmations and I believe these teachers have experienced the *Oneness* – or deep knowing – that I am talking about, and from that place of Oneness, they are sharing the words that resonate with their experience. If you have not experienced this Oneness, the act of affirming may seem to be missing something. People who have not found affirmations to be very helpful may have wondered what was wrong with them. I know that if we transform the constricting beliefs that stop us from seeing our true selves in all our glory, then affirmations confirm what we know to be true. They are not a desperate attempt to convince ourselves of something we **want** to be true.

Working on believing something may seem to make sense, but I came away with this insight from Dr. John Veltheim: **believing is simply not the same as knowing**. Over time, beliefs are going to change, often creating that old familiar feeling of standing on shifting ground. If our identity is tied up with what we do, or what we own, or who we share a relationship with, we will never feel safe because we have built our identity on shifting ground.

Knowing who we really are, and what our identity really is, creates a foundation so solid it cannot be budged. Dr. Veltheim pointed me in a direction that produced incredible results, and I give him a lot of credit. Once I realized how large and significant an impact this shift was having on me, I was very excited to see how it would work with my clients. The results have literally gone beyond my most ambitious expectations. Even clients find it hard to believe they have achieved results of such magnitude so quickly. I too was caught up in the energy of change and possibility. I could feel the pace accelerate and I personally was making big changes in my life.

By the spring of 2001 my life had changed radically. I moved from Calgary to Vancouver, British Columbia. This had an upside and a downside. The downside was that it was the straw that broke the camel's back for Wilma and me. Wilma was desperately homesick and wanted to return east to be with our grandkids, and I wanted to follow my dream of making a difference in the world. I love Prince Edward Island and it will always have a special place in my heart. I developed many of my skills there, it's where I started, but the prospects for building a global company were dismal. Vancouver was the place that held promise. I struggled desperately between wanting our married relationship to work and my deep knowing that Wilma and I wanted very different things from our lives and we were on very different paths. I knew I had something important to offer to the world and this meant following that passion wherever it led. The final decision to part was extremely difficult for us both, but in the end we knew it was for the best.

Happily, I can say that Wilma and I have remained on good terms and she is very close to all my family. When I returned home recently to attend my mother's funeral, Wilma joined our family in honoring Mom. This was a wonderful opportunity for coming full circle in many ways: saying goodbye to my Mom in an atmosphere of peace and acceptance and seeing Wilma happy in the environment she had chosen.

Very quickly I knew Vancouver was the right city where the company I was building could flourish. I enticed two colleagues to move to Vancouver to work with me – my associates and former mentors, Lynn Sumida and Steve Davis. They were willing to help me build a company that could reach out to the world. Excelanation™ Ltd. was founded to enhance the fundamental quality of life for all humanity.

The processes I developed were now fine-tuned into two streams, one for performance, called Excelability™, and the other for well-being and health, called Excelessence™. They were being road-tested in many new areas and we were getting very exciting results. Results like athletes winning gold medals and clients achieving personal goals in well-being and health.

At the Commonwealth Games in Nottingham, England, the Canadian rowing team I'd worked with initially won two gold medals and two silver medals and the following weekend won gold at the World University Rowing Championships. "Donn contributed by taking a team of contenders and making them champions in 10 weeks," said coach Mike Pearce.

In the health arena we were challenging the frontiers of spinal injuries, cancer and neurological ailments like Parkinson's disease. The critical issue was testing how far the body could go in repairing itself at the cellular level. I approached these illnesses and injuries from the perspective that the body can heal itself, if the constrictions in the system are removed. By holding onto the vision of optimal healing, the field was wide open to discover what the body, mind and spirit could really do. The exciting thing was we were already seeing results; our only question was how quickly and how deeply could the self-healing go?

I want to emphasize that I don't deal with the physical issues. That is the responsibility of the doctor. What I deal with is the imbalance in the person's system and the energy that is blocked. When you release the blocks, in most cases the symptoms dramatically diminish or disappear completely.

ILLNESSES RUN IN FAMILIES – OR DO THEY? THIS IS ANOTHER thought virus that is quite prevalent, and I was a firm believer myself for quite a few years. I thought alcoholism ran in families, and certainly had lots of proof of this. My grandfathers, my father, uncles, I and my son all suffered from alcoholism.

Then there were the migraine headaches. My grandmother had them, my Mom had them, I had them and my daughter Shelly had them. Once again it seemed to be genetic – something that ran in our family. Except, after I did some work on myself, my migraines stopped. Then I worked with Shelly and hers quit, too. Now I've changed my belief: I believe most symptoms are not genetic. Instead, what we pass down from generation to generation

are the thinking patterns. As I said earlier, how soon do you get wet when you go swimming? Whether you slip in inch-by-inch or dive in head-first, how soon are you wet? The answer is instantly, of course. It's the same with thought patterns. You are immersed in your parent's environment from conception. Yes, you can challenge that, but often we are not aware of how much we have actually accepted. How many of us, as new parents, were shocked to discover how much we had internalized our parent's style of parenting, even when we consciously vowed not to do this?

It is these thinking patterns that are passed from one generation to the next. In most cases, a symptom like migraine headaches is a pattern a person has learned at a subconscious level. It represents the body telling you that something is out of alignment. On the surface it can appear that something like chocolate causes a migraine headache. And on one level this is true. If my system is already at its maximum, one more thing can be the straw that breaks the camel's back. On a deeper level it is not the real cause. Underneath, there is some imbalance in the system that needs addressing. But many people are so relieved to identify a substance that seems to "cause" a migraine, they stop considering that there is a deeper issue to resolve. Once you resolve the underlying issues, symptoms like headaches or alcoholism can and do disappear. I say this because I have experienced it personally, and I have seen similar changes in many clients I have worked with.

I've spoken about the impact my alcoholism had on me and my family. The most devastating effect was the invisible one, the fears and constrictions that my daughter and son endured. Just like swimming, there was no way for them not to get wet or to be immune to the environment they lived in. I say this as a fact. But I want to stress to the reader that my feeling guilty or your feeling guilty is as useless as wishing you didn't have to get wet when you go swimming. It's just not possible. What we can do is strip away the illusions that prevent us from seeing the person we truly are on the inside. Once we do this others can see us as we truly are. I saw this in my daughter's face when she told the reporter I was a different man from the one she grew up with. Our personal change can profoundly influence others, including our children and their children.

Illness, and especially mental illness, has currently come under a lot of scrutiny. Films like *A Beautiful Mind* have opened up the question of how a pattern of coping really starts, however dysfunctional. Dr. Glasser challenged the whole idea of mental illness and mental health back in the '60s. Are mental illnesses really illnesses? Some people may wonder why it matters – what difference does it make? Well, it can make a big difference. Most people who believe they have an illness will take medication recommended by a doctor. The problem is medications that affect how the brain works have many side effects, not the least of which is the patient is no longer in charge of changes in the body; a chemical is now influencing that. Dr. Peter Breggin, in his books *Talking Back to Prozac**, *Talking Back to Ritalin** and *Your Drug May Be Your Problem**, speaks out strongly against medications. His books outline case after case where medications made the whole situation much worse. I am not a doctor and I cannot comment on what effects drugs have clinically on the brain. What I do know is this: the more a person understands that their body is a true reflection of what is going on emotionally and spiritually, the more they can take charge of their health. The more a person feels like a victim, in any way, the more they relinquish the power they have to change or heal.

* See bibliography

11

Leadership is creating a world to which
others want to belong.
ROBERT DILTS

THE EVENTS LEADING UP TO MY MOVE TO VANCOUVER ALMOST look like I planned the move. I certainly wasn't consciously doing this, but as they say, there are no coincidences. My last group in Calgary, in November 2000, was particularly memorable and contributed directly to the move. A woman named Debbie from Vancouver heard about my process and came to Calgary to participate. She was so pleased with her results she wanted others to learn about my work. She knew a gentleman who hosted a Vancouver radio talk show and offered to help get me on it. Needless to say, I was thrilled. I participated on the show in January and made a presentation the following week.

Out of the many who attended the presentation, one man stood out. He really understood what I was saying. He knew about going to higher levels of performance and marveled that it could happen so quickly. We agreed to meet the next day so he could take the process. He was in investor relations and had attended lots of personal growth seminars. He knew there was something different in what I was offering. He wanted to make some major shifts in his work and said if he got results, he had some close friends who would be very interested. Within three weeks his friends were ready to take the process. It seemed people in Vancouver were much more open to these ideas.

Word spread and I decided to stay in Vancouver a little longer. I was seeing clients in both provinces while I pondered which city was right for me. Moving to Vancouver was a big step, just as the move to Calgary was; it was an enormous change from the small city of Charlottetown, PEI. Growing up on an island, surrounded by water, I found I really missed the water the whole time I was in Calgary. I came to love the mountains, but I guess what they say is true – once an islander, always an islander. Vancouver, on the other hand, had water and mountains and a growing number of people who seemed interested in what I had to offer.

By the end of February, with my practice growing, I started to think of the Wholeness Center again. Yes, the dream was still alive; it had just gone into hibernation. I wanted and needed experienced people to work with me if I was ever going to grow beyond a one-man show and reach out on a global scale. My thoughts turned to Lynn Sumida, my former instructor and now a colleague. Lynn was still running a very successful private practice and she was also offering training around the world. I never knew whether she would be in Australia or South America when I'd call. Over the years I kept sharing my ideas with her as they evolved; I even tried to entice her to work with me in Calgary, but the timing just wasn't right. Each time we talked she raised the ultimate question, "Are clients still reversing the results and what is missing?" Lynn reflects:

> *In all my work with trauma and abuse the difficult issue wasn't the trauma, it was the self-sabotaging patterns that seemed to accompany these conditions. Because of the trauma, people learned ways to protect themselves from future hurt, and these coping*

strategies, in fact, became crippling to them. They were often afraid to trust, they would set boundaries that were too severe, or no boundaries at all. Ultimately, they were afraid of being too happy and too relaxed for fear of something going wrong. The concept of being a survivor became very popular and there was a huge ground-swell of groups that supported people moving out of victimhood to surviving. The problem is that surviving is quite different from living fully.

Even though I had co-developed a model for healing trauma and abuse, I was never satisfied with how we dealt with the self-sabotage patterns. Somehow we weren't getting at the root of what starts the pattern, nor how to fully release it from the system.

Donn continued to evolve in his understanding of self-sabotage and how people reverse the healthy changes they make. Donn's breakthrough came from studying his own self-sabotage patterns. He was relentless and just wouldn't give up. Finally, he found the way to locate the root of the self-sabotage pattern and how to dissolve it in the nervous system. This was the difference that allowed people to sustain the changes they made.

I knew my process was much more solid now; people were getting **and** maintaining results. I decided to call Lynn again and see if she would consider becoming part of a team in Vancouver. To my great surprise she promptly agreed to come out for a visit. She also suggested that Steve Davis, her long-time friend and colleague, might be interested in helping to "decode the recipe" of my new work. Steve is the trainer who taught me NLP and a former university professor. I admit I was quite choked up at the thought that he would be interested in helping me with my work. Now, two of my key teachers were willing to look at the process I had developed and help me take it to the next level. What an honor. Lynn recalls:

To really understand the enormous distance Donn travelled in his own growth, we need to go back 15 years, to when I first met him as that reluctant student, taking his first course in Reality Therapy, convinced he was going to fail – yet again. Over the years, he finished his training, and went on to other training programs, eating them up like they were candy. He became a voracious learner and everything he learned was grist for his mill. Donn was always on the hunt for the missing piece; we often joked about whether or not he was "looking for the Holy Grail" or the elixir of life. But, despite all the innovative ways he combined his ideas and strategies, some people were still sabotaging their progress. It didn't seem to matter what breakthroughs they had made, some people would shift the new patterns back to self-defeating ones.

I owned a private practice for 15 years and dealt with many clients addicted to food, alcohol, sex and relationships, who followed this same pattern of reversal. I was intrigued. Could we actually solve the puzzle of helping people attain lasting change, quickly and profoundly, and – if so – what was the key?

One time when Donn was passing through Manitoba he stopped for a visit and showed me how he was combining all the pieces he had learned in a whole new way. Suddenly I knew – he's onto something. That was 1995. It would take another five years of work before Donn would solve the riddle of how to help people stop sabotaging themselves.

In the meantime we kept in touch. Donn moved to Calgary and kept me posted on new techniques he developed, but the question was always: How long will it take before the client starts to undo it? In February of 2000, when I got his call saying, "I really think I've got the process now," there was something very different in his voice. I knew this was the time and agreed to come out and take a look. And I wanted Steve Davis, a fellow international trainer, to join us because Steve and I work very differently. I knew we would make a great team. It was an exhilarating five days. We charged full speed ahead, seeing clients, experiencing the new process ourselves and videotaping everything.

I think it's important to say that Steve and I have worked on our own personal development and growth since the late '70s. We believe in it, and see it as our professional responsibility to address our own internal work. We both knew what issues we had worked on successfully, what was solid and what hadn't shifted.

It was thrilling to see Donn work with Steve. Steve would say he was a person who was very quick to judge. He had worked hard to soften that side of himself, adding humor and compassion, but that streak was still there, almost as strong as ever. After working with Donn, it shifted dramatically. He finally connected with what had started the pattern, and made the shift at a core level. He got to the essence of who he is and who he wants to be. The caring, sensitive, compassionate person, who was always there, was now in full view, every day.

I also had a very profound experience working with Donn. I believed I had high self-esteem. I have close friends and family; I've been extremely fortunate, getting jobs I wanted and doing work I love. I am also one of five adopted children. So, over the years I did a lot of work on the issue of feeling wanted and lovable. I believed I'd addressed these issues and would have argued with anybody who said I hadn't.

After a major crisis in my life, I realized I needed to take another look at my self-esteem and my inner core. I was feeling a lot of stress and pressure; I could actually see the hairline crack in my emotional foundation and how deeply it ran. I was devastated by this and wanted to deal with the source and the damage once and for all. Donn was the first person I thought of to help me. I knew this wasn't something I could do for myself. It would be like trying to go into your own system to remove layers of protection you put there in the first place; your system is going to fight you all the way.

My first comment to Donn was, "Don't even think it's about being lovable. I've examined that from here to eternity and it's been dealt with." In his wonderful manner, he said OK, and within five minutes we're deep in that issue and I'm crying away, saying I can't believe that's the issue.

Donn didn't focus on the pain just to help me feel better; he wanted to get to the source of where the whole process of not valuing "me" started. It's one thing to know something intellectually – it started when my birth mother gave me up – and it's another matter to transform an issue embedded in your nervous system. I discovered I had not removed the trauma surrounding my abandonment at birth. In all my previous work I really hadn't reached the core of the issue or reconnected fully with myself. I still had doubts about how lovable I was. This is what shifted when I worked with Donn – and the impact was life changing.

Another unique aspect of Donn's process is the speed of change. As a counselor, I know how to get to know someone well and pinpoint issues. But to not only see issues and coping patterns identified, watch people taking ownership for their behavior, and see energy blocks being transformed at the nervous system level – all in three hours – that's very different. This process involved more than just dealing with a buried emotion. It addresses the whole way you've constructed your world.

I don't think everybody wants to make changes like these. Courage is definitely required. Most of us have to get to a place where there is some sense of urgency, where the discomfort is strong enough. This discomfort can be "I'm not who I want to be or am capable of being" or "I just can't stand another day of looking in the mirror and feeling this way." When you get rid of the blocks or the ways you stop yourself from truly being as wonderful as you are –

smart, funny, creative – you are not only more relaxed, funnier and more loving, you're healthier, too.

Fifteen years later, Donn's process had evolved to the point where Steve and I both knew his work was pivotal and terribly important for the world, given the challenges facing humanity. We were thrilled to have the opportunity to help him expand his work by analyzing the process, training others and building a company that would make a difference in the world.

IN MARCH, WHEN LYNN AND STEVE FLEW OUT TO VANCOUVER, we spent a glorious week together. They both experienced the new process and were thrilled with their personal results. They videotaped me working with clients and holding follow-up sessions, and we broke the process down into its major components. The million-dollar question was: Could other trainers, starting with my associates, use my process and get the same results? If not, this would be a major stumbling block for expansion. By the end of the week Lynn and Steve felt certain they could duplicate the process and they flew back to Manitoba to road-test it. The great news is they could duplicate it and were able to help clients get significant results quickly. Steve shares his thoughts:

The trip to Vancouver to spend time with Donn Smith was a landmark occasion for me. His timing was perfect. I was feeling stagnant in my own work and was ripe for discovering what he had developed that was new. I was a psychology professor, a veteran of many personal growth and development approaches, and an internationally recognized NLP trainer – all because of my life's dream: finding ways to assist people in having richer and fuller lives, ones in which they are able to realize their fullest potential. After over 20 years of using NLP with clients (it was an approach that surpassed any other I had discovered), my clients would achieve major and lasting, life-altering transformations about five times

out of a hundred. I knew more was not only possible, but essential.
With challenges in daily living increasing so rapidly in every
aspect of life, it was apparent to me there is an absolutely crucial
need for people to develop more resiliency and to overcome internal
limitations more rapidly than ever before.

Donn had taken the NLP Practitioner training from me in
1992 and the Master Practitioner training in 1994. I knew he was
developing his own unique combination of skills and I had observed
him from afar. In early 2001, when Donn Smith made the call to
Lynn, and she called me, it was an opportunity I couldn't resist.
Observing him using his approach and then experiencing it myself,
I knew this was exactly the next step I was yearning for. My dream
and passion for working with people was rekindled. With his new
process Donn Smith's clients were making major breakthroughs 90
per cent of the time. I was determined to find out what he was doing
in his work that was so significantly new and different. Clearly, the
student had surpassed the teacher and the opportunity to learn
from him was one I relished.

12

A person's interpretations of the environment
as safe or threatening, based on beliefs developed
in childhood, become internal signals
that lead cells to generate the response.

BRUCE LIPTON

WHILE STEVE AND LYNN WERE BACK IN MANITOBA TESTING the process, I continued my research for the most direct way to help people access this *knowing*. Like finding the combination to a safe, I knew most of the numbers, but I thought one or two were still missing and I wasn't sure which sequence was optimal. Like the Rubik's Cube, every time I changed one link, it impacted the others, but gradually it was all coming together. The goal was to assist people in reaching the state of knowing and tapping into their capacity to live in that place of peace and connection. My earlier experience of completely releasing all the pain and anguish I felt over losing baby Mary, only to be filled instantly with peace and gratitude, was a blueprint I knew was possible for all human beings. It was this experience that convinced me huge changes were possible and could be made almost instantaneously. Yet, how to do this intentionally remained a mystery.

Remember when I was offered the job of building the 18-story high-rise? The first thing I did was to reject the offer, when I had been praying for something to improve in my life. I'd been dreaming about being a foreman and, as soon as I got a chance, I rejected it. The second thing I did was panic when I didn't have all the answers right away. This totally immobilized me at precisely the time I needed my wits about me. I was a perfect example of sabotage in action! Here I had a chance to go in the direction of my passion and instead I go the opposite way. At the cellular level I later realized I was giving a double message to my system all the time. No wonder my confused cells didn't know which direction to take. Where was the blueprint now? Clearly, one experience of peace was not enough to release all the constrictions in my system.

One of the things in my favor was my enormous curiosity: I had to ask why? Why was I indulging in all this crazy behavior? I had to look beyond the symptoms to the root cause. Clearly I still had trauma still locked in my nervous system – that was why I went into panic mode on the high-rise job, as if a tiger was attacking me. My next step was to find a way to dissolve the trauma of past events that still haunted my nervous system. I knew that limiting beliefs, like I am stupid, unloved, bad, stem from early traumas. If I could dissolve the traumas, the limiting beliefs should transform as well. But the real challenge was to deal with trauma more deeply than just intellectually. Otherwise the trauma remains in the system, only your understanding of it changes. And the changes in your beliefs, made at the intellectual level, will likely at some point reverse. Let me give you an example. I worked with a woman who had experienced a great deal of pain in her relationship with her father. He was quite a harsh person when it came to discipline and sharing what he believed was "right and wrong." Over the years this woman felt she hated her father because of how he behaved. Because this pain never really went away she was on the lookout for anything that might make a difference. One day, as an adult she was introduced to the idea of forgiveness: that the only way out of her pain was to forgive him and move on. She proceeded to work on forgiving him and finally felt that she had. She shifted her beliefs about herself from "I am worthless, stupid and unattractive" to more positive ones "I am a good person, people value me and I value me and I know I am competent." All of this, by the way, was many years ago.

When we met and I asked her what she wanted to achieve she expressed a number of goals, none of them having anything to do with her father. This issue was resolved as far as she was concerned. The irony of this is that the hurt and pain of her early experiences was still locked in her nervous system. How could I tell this?

Two things told me the trauma wasn't gone. One, she was still attracting the same pattern of abusive relationship in her life, and two, when I asked direct questions about her father, there was still a strong emotional response. When we began exploring her ability to take risks in other areas of her life, she immediately was on guard; she became tense and even a little defensive. Her fear of being criticized, failing, etc. was as strong as ever and directly linked to her early experiences with her father. When I checked her system using kinesiology, the trauma was still locked in her nervous system. The kinesiology test was not for me, but more to help her see that the trauma was still locked in her system. Intellectually she had resolved the issue with her father, but she didn't have the tools to dissolve it in her nervous system.

Just working on beliefs will not build a foundation that is solid. I realized my work with people was just that: building on sand and the ground was still trembling under my feet. I needed to go deeper and this finally led me to the realization of what was the root cause of people's distress.

Before I talk about the root cause I would like to comment on the difference between change at the intellectual level and change at the cellular level. Caroline Myss, in her book *Anatomy of the Spirit** and her tapes *Energy Anatomy**, outlines an amazing framework for understanding ourselves. I really appreciate her framework. Likewise, Gary Zukav's powerful and

* See bibliography

heartfelt book *Seat of Soul** addresses profound issues. But, using only the intellect, I think there are limitations on how far and how quickly you will progress. This is not to say you won't make progress, and it's not meant to put down intellectual understanding. I am in awe of great thinkers who can articulate wonderful ideas and illuminate them for all of us to see. Many of these writers have given people the encouragement to keep moving and searching and these are invaluable steps in the process of self-discovery.

But to return to *Seat of the Soul*, as Gary says, if you "choose to feel kindness instead of coldness, you change the frequency of your consciousness and this changes your experiences." I agree and I would add that if there are emotional wounds underneath, a person will not be able to sustain this new consciousness. Unfortunately, what often follows is a pattern of feeling badly or beating up on ourselves for failing to maintain what we know to be optimum. In *The Power of Now**, Eckhart Tolle brilliantly describes the power of being in the present. The challenge, of course, is staying in the now. Many people are not able to stay in the now – and what pulls them out of the now is fear. This fear is linked to early experiences that are stored at the cellular level. You cannot arbitrarily override this fear. Any attempts can lead you into playing out the pattern I described as self-reliance, which is not the same as true peace. And you can't meditate these fears away. I have worked with people who have spent years meditating and have an amazing ability to distance themselves from the fear. But the fear never really leaves their nervous system.

So ever on the lookout for clues and missing pieces to this amazing puzzle I was working on, I heard about a program that helps a person move to higher levels of consciousness. The program was called Crystal Mastery Training, and what caught my attention was the word **crystal**. Dr. Bruce Lipton, a cellular biologist who worked at Stanford, talks about our cell lining being made of crystal. I was very interested in cellular structure and how cells change. Could there be a connection between Crystal Mastery

* See bibliography

Training and the cellular changes I was interested in?

Dr. Lipton explains: The cell membrane is primarily composed of "phospholipids" and proteins. Phospholipids, which resemble lollipops with two sticks, are arranged in a crystalline bilayer. A biochemical definition describes the cell membrane: the membrane is a *liquid crystal* (phospholipid organization) *semiconductor* (the only things that can cross the membrane barrier are those brought across by transport IMPs – Integral Membrane Proteins) *with gates* (receptor IMPs) *and channels* (effector IMPs). This terminology matches the language used to define a computer chip. Recent studies have verified that the cell membrane is in fact an organic *homologue* of a silicon chip. That means it has a similar structure, but not the same function. Studies on cloned human cells led me to the awareness that the cell's *plasmalemma*, commonly referred to as the *cell membrane*, represents the cell's "brain."

Although I can't say I fully understand the scientific implications of Dr. Lipton's explanation, two things are significant for me: one is our cells have a crystal lining and the other is the brain of the cell is situated in the membrane, meaning the membrane does the work of evaluating information as it comes in. This confirmed my insight that how we perceive the environment is what determines what the cells do, instead of the popular idea that our DNA predetermines how a cell will respond. If we perceive the environment as dangerous, we will go into protective mode, including at the cellular level; if we feel safe and loved, we will be open to growth. My goal was to help people remove all emotional wounds that could trigger our cells going into protection mode, so that we could sustain a constant feeling of safety and peace. Now in case you are thinking it is essential to survival that we do go into protection mode, you are of course right. I want to differentiate between briefly going into protective mode and the extended protective mode we go into when we feel emotionally unsafe. My observation is that most people feel a level of un-safety all the time. This produces the cumulative stress that is so hard on our bodies and yet is invisible. As Dr. Lipton says, our cells are designed to go into protective mode, but they are not designed to stay there for long periods of time. Needless to say, I signed up for the Crystal Mastery Training, to experience, first hand, what it offered.

Crystal Mastery Training involves a great deal of meditation, which was already an integral part of my life. In my daily routine, I meditate for one to two hours each morning when I wake up, about 5 a.m. In the program we meditated for much longer periods and this definitely opened up new levels for me. It felt like I was dissolving ice that surrounded the core of my being and melting away some of the protection I'd built up. The *developed ego* feeds on fear, past, present or future, and drives us to layer on more protection in the form of self-reliance or dependency.

This layer needs to be dissolved first, before peace and oneness can emerge. This training brought me closer to my destination, that place of knowing, because I was less blocked by constricting energy. I was less anxious, fearful and worried, and I became more trusting in all areas of my life.

THE CRYSTAL MASTER TRAINING

The Crystal Master Training, developed by Christa Faye Burka, is a life-long development process that calls for a clear commitment to a person's own personal and professional growth. There is a remarkable intelligence within this energy that seems to bring each Crystal Master into their unique form of expression with the crystal energy.

Many plants have medicinal and therapeutic benefits for humankind. The same is true for the mineral kingdom. Natural quartz crystal works directly with the human consciousness to assist in raising it to a higher energetic frequency or vibration. The primary focus of Crystal Mastery Training is to connect directly and profoundly with the essence of crystal energy and to awaken our deep inner crystal consciousness.

After the training, my effectiveness with clients really accelerated and my process became much more refined. I suddenly realized what to change to take the bulkiness out of the process. It became a smoother, deeper and more elegant process. I had one more of the missing numbers to the combination for the safe and it fit together beautifully with everything else. I now knew how to reverse the self-sabotage pattern: you not only had to dissolve the trauma in the cellular system, re-establish an awareness of the connection to the spirit; you had to help the conscious mind understand why all the behaviors we used were attempts to get what we needed. If you don't do this, people start picking apart the changes they have made. You may laugh – but people have said everything from "I feel too good, it can't be this easy" to "This was too quick." And these are the same people who had already spent years trying to make changes and who said they were ready to really go for it all.

Many forms of technology today are designed to make things lighter and more streamlined. Computers are smaller, lighter, ski equipment is more aerodynamic and race cars are just plane faster. The goals are still the same, but by reducing bulk and using new materials in new combinations, the result is a lighter, more streamlined, efficient product. So by reducing, less actually becomes more. Steve Davis said that the difference in the process from March to October 2001, seven months later, was like "going from a Model-T Ford to a Lamborghini."

13

For one human being to love another;
that is perhaps the most difficult of all our tasks,
the ultimate, the last test and proof,
the work for which all other work is but preparation.
RAINER MARIA RILKE, 1875 – 1926

I'VE ALWAYS BELIEVED THAT WORKING WITH COUPLES PRESENTED exciting possibilities for personal growth and enhanced intimacy. The first group to experience the new process in Vancouver included a couple who would test these ideas. Now that I had refined my focus, I was fired up and ready to move ahead.

Ellen and her husband Derek, two of the participants, are seasoned veterans of alternative methods of healing. Both are Reiki Masters, an ancient form of Japanese healing, and they study with a Shaman. Unfortunately, true to the stereotype of many caregivers, they admitted to neglecting to care for themselves. Ellen was coping with fibromyalgia. Three years earlier she had a serious car accident, resulting in chronic pain, loss of strength and physical ability. The excruciating pain and muscle weakness left her without enough strength to drive a car. Derek also wanted to make changes in his life. He felt that unresolved issues of being abused as a child were keeping him from making progress in many areas of his life. So both Ellen and Derek were keen to try something new. Working with me fascinated them because I work with the body's energy and nervous system.

"I already knew if you made changes right at the nervous system level, you are able to make shifts [in your behavior] with less effort," Derek said. Ellen was intrigued by the concept of unblocking energy, so that "you were allowed to be as you truly are."

I was delighted to have a couple in the group. I have long believed that if couples evolve together, it enriches the relationship beyond description. Do you remember the training I went through with Dr. Harville Hendricks? One of the things I believed then, and still believe, is that couples can reach a high level of intimacy without spending years in therapy. The key is they **both** need to shed the layers of developed ego. My process is so powerful that if one person changes profoundly, it has serious ramifications for the relationship. A good example is Richard and Gayle, the couple who dealt with grief. Gayle died of cancer, but before she did her life changed dramatically over the 18 months we knew each other – and so did Richard's. Gayle found the peace that had eluded her all her life. Richard shares what it was like having his partner make a quantum leap ahead and how he felt.

"Donn was at a conference I organized when Gayle revealed to him that the cancer had returned. He offered to work with her immediately. This was the first time Gayle had worked with Donn and she addressed many issues she had wrestled with for a long time, one of which was spirituality. Gayle did not want to follow her mother's example. Her Mum's spirituality was entwined with religion – and that didn't fit. Gayle's solution was to close the door and avoid the whole issue. While working with Donn, Gayle had the profound realization she was the only one in charge of her spirituality. This had an enormous impact. So much so that one of the very last things she expressed was that she was completely healed – she meant at the deepest level of her being. Her physical health faded as a focus completely.

"After Gayle worked with Donn, I was completely over the edge with how Gayle had grown; I felt threatened, even with all I knew about the process. It is overwhelming to see someone, with whom you feel you are *one*, launch forward. She moved forward so dramatically it felt like a Cape Canaveral moon-shot. She became someone who was not burdened with fears or regrets and was ready to make changes, big time. I wasn't ready for that. We are not raised to think of changing so dramatically. I literally called Donn up and said: 'I don't know what your plans are for the next few days, but you have to fit me in somewhere.' Of course, Donn did and it was wonderful."

In relationships we attract people who push our own buttons. The pain, resulting from our buttons being pushed, is one of the ways we identify constrictions in our system, that we have so craftily camouflaged. We all know what this feels like. Let's say you are interacting with someone and suddenly a seemingly innocent conversation takes a nosedive and you become very upset over a comment. This is an opportunity to look at the deeper issues that lie underneath. For example, an individual with a fear of abandonment might take the slightest remark about "not doing something together" as a sign of rejection. If you have a wound around feeling valued or worthwhile, then anything that relates to this issue could push that magic button. Most people put their effort into controlling others so their own buttons don't get pushed. And if they do get pushed, they go into blaming rather than exploring what the sensitivity is all about. Ironically, having our buttons pushed is an **opportunity** for us to identify and resolve core issues and this is precisely why we attracted the person in the first place.

In relationships two people's patterns are interacting. For example, a person who is afraid of intimacy will constantly want space or freedom. They will perceive situations or actions as their partner "smothering" them and will want to find ways to create distance. The other partner will experience the distancing as a form of abandonment and constantly feel they are being "rejected." Life mirrors what is inside of us. So if I grew up in a family where people were not close, I will likely attract a partner who has trouble with true intimacy.

In addition to this pattern, I have identified another component. Using fear of intimacy as an example, I would like you to think of a 25-cent coin. It has two sides, one with heads, the other tails, but it is the same coin. The issue of intimacy is one side of the coin and the other side is the fear of abandonment. They are the two sides of the same coin, only one side is in our conscious awareness and the other is much more hidden.

I discovered this when I started looking at the patterns of how Wilma and I interacted. My fear of abandonment was what I was most aware of. I never felt Wilma loved me enough. There were only four times in 30 years that I could recall a fear of being smothered. So of course I thought this wasn't an issue for me! Wrong. The reason there were only four examples was not because it wasn't an issue for me, it was that I picked a person who wasn't comfortable being openly affectionate with her love. This meant the issue rarely came up. But the fact that four times stand out for me when I remember having the emotional response of feeling smothered told me the fear was in my system.

It is the objective of a relationship to resolve these "wounds" we carry over from our childhood. And they will keep showing up in our relationships until they are resolved. **Unfortunately we have a phobic response to meeting the very need we so desperately want to fill.** How is this possible, when it seems to make no sense? The knowledge that all behavior is purposeful is what kept me trying to understand this pattern. Finally I did. In a nutshell, I realized that because of traumatic earlier experiences, we feel vulnerable. We believe we could be hurt again, so we go into panic mode at the mere thought of getting what we really want. We believe we could lose it or get too much or be smothered again. This would be so painful that, unconsciously, we make sure we don't get what we want. When we are not in panic mode the sensitivity is still there; we just remain in neutral, with our system scanning for when to activate the button.

The ideal solution is to resolve these issues as a couple. Let me explain. If one individual resolves their "rejection" issue and all of a sudden stops worrying about anyone leaving them, they will begin to behave very differently. They will likely not be so smothering in their behavior because the fear of rejection is gone. Their partner will sense this change and may become afraid, deep down, that they will be abandoned. This fear will only rise to the surface once their partner is no longer smothering them. This is why we are often unaware of the other side of the coin. But there are always two sides to our wounds: one side is conscious (in our awareness) and one is unconscious (outside our awareness).

Just in case someone reading this is not in an intimate relationship and thinks they have escaped this conundrum, think again. These patterns show up in relationships with our bosses or friends or colleagues. If we look back over our lives, we will see a recurring pattern that continues until it is resolved at the source. In Imago Relationship Therapy, Dr. Hendricks describes how couples are attracted to each other based on the patterns they experienced growing up, modeled by significant caregivers. This matches what I call *living with the familiar.* Many of us have vowed not to be like our parents and yet, people repeat these patterns either as parents or partners. These patterns are so familiar they become part of our overall nervous system. When we address them at the *source,* where they were created, we can quickly make changes without spending years in therapy. Many people have fallen prey to the great myth that "it's just my personality" to act a certain way. Many coping patterns – such as being negative or pessimistic, not being affectionate, being addicted to self-dramatization – camouflage who we really are. If people can address these issues, they often find, as Sherry did in chapter eight, "a wonderful, life-loving person" inside. Derek and Ellen were both surprised when they looked within.

In the group, Derek and Ellen had the special opportunity of sharing each other's journey and growth. This, by the way, was a huge commitment on their part. Financially, they were not in a position for even one of them to attend; but they made a decision, set their priorities and just kept working at finding the finances. I loved seeing them stay open to the possibilities of what can happen, not letting doubt in and trusting the universe to provide. This is so easy to say – and absolutely true – but hard to carry out.

The process for Ellen and Derek was very powerful. Derek was able to open what was locked inside, transform the pain and hurt, and emerge connected to his true essence. Ellen discovered her symptoms were a result of a deep sense of not feeling lovable. "I learned so much more about myself," she said. "I've helped so many people in my life, and to turn around and realize I wasn't feeling loved [in return] shocked me. I also found doing the process with four others was very profound. What it boils down to is every person has similar problems – they just manifest themselves in different ways."

The first phase for the group took place over a weekend. At the end of the weekend Ellen made a startling announcement: she was strong enough to drive home. And she did. Because of her previous car accident, Ellen hadn't been able to drive for three years. She drove the two-hour trip home and hasn't looked back since. "To me this was colossal. I've driven a car since I was 16, driving is really important to me; and for three years, relying on someone else was really tough. What a huge gift to be able to drive again."

Derek comments on his changes: "The process transformed my perceptions… helping me take responsibility for my own life and knowing I can create what I want. Donn's process gave me the confidence to be responsible for myself. He opened both of us up to changing our own lives."

Previously Derek spent a great deal of his life just coping. What do I mean by coping? Like survival, it's keeping our heads above water. I know a lot about this because for most of my life I used coping skills to survive, to cover up my insecurities. I was hoping no one would see just how insecure I was. This hiding is one of the reasons why a lot of individuals don't take part in such a powerful process. They are afraid the issues they have been hiding subconsciously will be visible and all the defense mechanisms they have built up over the years will fall apart and they will be totally exposed.

This in fact does happen, with one exception: it isn't scary like their developed ego has convinced them it will be. As a matter of fact, there is such relief as the system returns to its natural state that many people end up laughing at all the behaviors they have used to keep their lives together.

Remember when the kid punched me in the nose in grade three? Until that incident, I coped by fighting my way through life. I covered up how scared I was and beat everybody else up. From the single experience of being hit hard, I completely changed how I got along in the world. I went from very, very aggressive to very, very passive.

I did the same thing when I was afraid to ask a girl to dance. Having a drink of alcohol made all of the fears, anxieties, worries and doubts recede. I had all this false confidence: coping at its finest. Alcohol, like fighting or passive victimhood, was a way to deal with life; it took care of all the fears and inadequacies I kept inside.

The difficulty with coping is that our system stays stuck in the pattern – it's like never actually passing grade one. I might be put into grades two, three, four and five, but I was still stuck back at grade one. Like an LP record that keeps skipping, I was repeating the same passage over and over.

The face of coping mechanisms may change from the two-year-old throwing a temper tantrum, to the 28-year-old who's fighting in the bar, or the 40-year-old who's screaming and yelling at their partner, but the pattern is the same. People are using familiar patterns to cope with a situation; they don't solve anything, they just keep repeating. Attempts to change relationships, bosses or friends rarely work. As we attract people into our lives, they keep triggering the wounds we have hidden. We don't want to look at those wounds because when they happened, they were too painful and we didn't know how to handle them. So we "cope" instead.

If you think about the story of the dead skin on my hands after I got burned, the dead skin is like coping – trying to deal with the sensitivity inside and covering it up. When you take the old dead skin off, the new skin is sensitive for a few days, but the natural, healthy skin will quickly feel normal if given a chance. When we use coping mechanisms, we never strip off the outer layer and connect with our natural, authentic state. If we refuse to remove the "dead skin," the new skin never has a chance to breathe and become strong. A lot of our behavior, including dealing with emotional issues, physical illnesses and injuries, involves some form of coping mechanism, obscuring areas of our lives that are out of balance and not in harmony.

However, when we are authentic, with nothing to hide, there is an energy about us. Others recognize it, feel it, see it; it's very real. There is no phoniness. The authenticity comes through in our voice, our body posture, even our way of walking. You can't hide anything that beautiful.

The problem is people do not always want to give up their coping mechanisms. Fear keeps them trapped in familiar patterns.

Coping has so many faces: people with eating disorders, an athlete who's broken every record known to man, someone with chronic fatigue, fibromyalgia or arthritis, a little girl who has a rash, or the person who breaks into a blind rage every once in a while. I believe these are all are attempts to deal with life, to cope. Still, once your body is in distress the pain is very real. No one sits down and says, "I think I'll get this illness or that problem."

These coping mechanisms are often addressed intellectually. What I mean by this is people are often assisted in understanding a situation and taking actions that seem to fit, like forgiving a person, using affirmations, prayer, rituals, etc.

However, if you know where the symptoms come from, the cause behind them, and how to change the patterns neurologically, then the patterns and the symptoms can truly dissolve. For example, a client with no effort, no special diet, lost 40 pounds in one month. When key issues were resolved, his body didn't need the extra weight to protect him anymore, so it naturally came off. He no longer needed to cope with life by adding a layer of fat. The beautiful thing was he made the change without conscious effort. When we are authentic we can deal with issues, people, places and situations in ways that are natural and flowing, much like breathing.

Ellen was addressing this point exactly when she expressed how wonderful it was "...to be as you truly are." Her physical recovery was just a side benefit when she connected to her true essence and allowed all the energy to flow through her body without constriction.

Working with Derek and Ellen was really enjoyable, inpart because they were a couple. When it comes to working with couples, my ideal situation is to work with them early in the relationship. So many patterns are established in the beginning stages. When a couple can clear or avoid limiting patterns early in the relationship and connect from their true essence, the foundation they build will be incredible. Kevin and Sabrina, another couple I wanted to tell you about, were in the early stages of building their relationship when we worked together.

I HAVE YET TO SEE ANYONE MAKE A DECISION ABOUT TAKING this process as fast as Kevin. He listened to me for five minutes, asked three questions, and said, "I'm in." When he asked me how soon we could get started and I named the day and the time, he said, "I'll be there." First thing the next morning I got a phone call from him. "My partner saw the Preparation Form last night and would like to take the process with me. Can I bring her along?" I said yes, and that was the beginning of working with Kevin and Sabrina.

Although the decision-making was easy for Kevin, what was going on underneath was quite different. "I went into the process a little cautiously; in fact I looked Donn in the eye and said: I've been to a hundred programs. What makes you think your program is going to last longer than two weeks? None of the others did." As Kevin recalls this, he laughs, "Donn likes to remind me of that, even a year later!

"Just before seeing Donn I sold my company, SportMart, and this was very scary for me. For most of the 17 years that I owned the company, it represented who I was. Selling it was devastating. I felt a huge loss and

I was really searching for who I was, without this thing that defined me," says Kevin. "I've spent a lot of years reading the books and seeing people. I've always been fascinated with improving myself mentally, so Donn just seemed like another chapter in bettering myself."

"It's funny about successful people, we look at them and think there are no flaws. We look at this façade and believe that individual is happy, content, cruising through life with no effort. It looks like they are enjoying all the challenges and successes, and just taking it all in stride. The reality is that's not the case. Internally, there's a lot of turmoil – successful people have just gotten really good at masking the fears that haunt them."

Sabrina and Kevin had been dating for less than a year when they experienced the process. Sabrina comments, "It helped so much with our relationship because it opened everything up. It was like – here I am and this is what I'm all about; I shared all my fears and insecurities. Donn helped bring everything to the surface and doing that in front of one another, in a new relationship, was really something."

I told them it was incredibly brave of both of them to open up so honestly in front of each other, especially at such an early stage in their relationship. Kevin's reply was: "It came down to why not? If we really feel this strongly about one another and are serious about being together, why not let it all hang out together? It was awesome to learn about one another, we both got to see why each of us reacts the way we do – or maybe overreacts sometimes – what the meaning is behind a lot of things we do and say."

Sabrina added, "Many people don't know who they are and what their purpose is in life. More than that, they never sit back and ask themselves those questions. With Donn's help we discovered the answers inside ourselves. It's kind of like an inner revelation. The process gives you a greater understanding of yourself and of the universe. It happened on a spiritual level, but it was not religious. Donn brought a lot of things to my attention that I would not normally think about. I found myself saying: 'Why haven't I thought of this before, or why do I care about that?'"

As Kevin said, he was at a crossroads in his life. "I already had tremendous success on the professional side, but I was at a place in my life where, for the first time, I was focusing more on my personal life. And quite frankly, it's where I needed the most improvement. I'd left it on the backburner too long. My teeter-totter was vertical, that's how unbalanced I was, and now I was committed to change."

Kevin continues: "I am blown away by the number of people who invest huge amounts of money in improving their health physically through training and fitness clubs. They're determined to make themselves better, but they fail to grasp that it starts with the brain. **Investing in your mental health is a prerequisite, not just a recommendation.** I don't know anybody who wouldn't benefit significantly from some sort of mental tune-up. Speaking of health – how's this for a statement of support for the program: When I was 20 years old I started getting hives. I went through all the tests to find what I was allergic to when, finally, my doctor said they're stress-related.

"I'd get them so often, I used a drug for 15 years to prevent them. Recently, I switched to an herb. Two weeks after taking Phase II with Donn, I mentioned my hives. He said what often happens is the medication interferes with the body finding its own solution. Once the energy blocks are removed from your system, the system can rebalance itself and in many cases the symptoms disappear. That was a year ago and I've had maybe five attacks since. I would normally have a thousand – this to me is mind blowing, especially considering I was not taking any medication."

I would like to add to what I said to Kevin. Many people are speaking out courageously about the impact of chemicals on the human system. Dr. Peter Breggin addressed this in his book *Your Drug May Be Your Problem**. Twenty-five years ago he founded The International Center for the Study of Psychiatry and Psychology (ICSPP), an organization dedicated to "informing professionals, media and the public about the potential dangers of drugs, electroshock, psychosurgery and the biological theories

* See bibliography

155

of psychiatry."* The human system has an innate ability to heal itself and I feel we have hardly begun to scratch the surface of this ability. Not only does our body have a tremendous capacity to heal, we can also influence natural processes like ageing. The renowned author, Deepak Chopra M.D., writes about the incredible impact beliefs have on aging in his groundbreaking book *Ageless Body, Timeless Mind.**

Because we view aging as a disease, we have created a box that most of us are stuck in. The same applies to all aspects of our health and well-being. We have not tapped into our abilities to regenerate and heal because we have not believed this to be possible, and we have not had the human change technology to deal with the energy constrictions in our system. Now we do and can.

Physical change was only one of the benefits Kevin gained. He continues, "The single most enlightening thing for me was the way it fast-tracked my ability to focus on the strengths that existed in me, strengths that had nothing to do with what I had accomplished or what those accomplishments previously represented to me as a person."

Kevin feels it was the best decision he and Sabrina ever made. "We've built a foundation not just for ourselves, but as a couple. It was awesome – we are really, really strong as a couple now." Since getting married this past spring, Kevin and Sabrina renovated a house and traveled extensively. "It's been a totally crazy year, but we've sailed through it," Sabrina says. "Compared to all the other relationships both Kevin and I have had, this has taken us to a level we've never experienced before."

Working with individuals, couples, families and communities to be healthy and strong is how I hope to be instrumental in building a more loving world for everyone. Person by person, couple by couple and family by family, we **can** reach around the globe.

* See bibliography

14

What lies behind us and what lies before us are tiny matters
compared to what lies within us.
RALPH WALDO EMERSON, 1803 – 1882

GETTING TO KNOW KEVIN REMINDED ME OF MANY ISSUES I HAD
dealt with. I understood his incredible success and the price he paid for it,
and I identified with his self-reliance, something I struggled with for years.
I would like to clarify what self-reliance means to me. I know many people
see it as a wonderful quality; parents often push their children to have
more of it – the old stand-on-your-own-two-feet philosophy. And yet when
I examined it closely within myself, I discovered weakness, not strength;
another coping pattern.

When I shifted out of feeling the victim – a victim of poverty, lack of
love, failure at school – I moved into self-reliance. I started down the road
of becoming the 'self-made man.' As productive as this phase of my growth
was, it was not the ultimate destination. I would eventually discover what
lay beyond self-reliance. In discussions with Lynn and Steve it was clear that
I was addressing the issue of dependency on self versus dependency on others

taught in psychology and counseling programs. I didn't learn it there but found it, first hand, in my behavior and the behavior of people all around me. It was epidemic! The difference was I wanted to go far beyond labeling the patterns and get at the root of what starts the pattern so that it could effectively be reversed. But let me tell you first about how I believe self-reliance develops.

Being overly self-reliant has been a personal limitation of mine for many years. Remember my vivid memory of lying in the crib, grabbing for a rope suspended in mid-air? That panic locked into my nervous system as did a deep-seated wariness, an ongoing expectation that something terrible was going to happen. These were the messages I took from that experience, the panic or phobia that I call *trauma*. Traumas cause untold damage to our cells; we constrict our energy when we feel threatened. That's a lot of damage, since we have 50 to 70 trillion cells in our bodies.

Dr. Gabor Mate, author of *Scattered Minds – A New Look at the Origins and Healing of Attention Deficit*, gives one example of the significance of the environment and the impact of trauma: "Of all environments, the one that most profoundly shapes the human personality is the invisible one: the emotional atmosphere in which the child lives during the critical early years of brain development… Psychological tension in the parents' lives during the child's infancy is, I am convinced, a major and universal influence on the subsequent emergence of ADD."

From the moment I experienced trauma, I had a gigantic need to control everything in my surroundings; I clung to self-reliance in an attempt to get that happy, peaceful, safe feeling back. But this self-reliance is not a natural state of balance; it was my desperate attempt to gain control and it pushed everyone I loved away. My strong religious background, one with a God of hellfire and damnation, created even greater fear and need for control. Basically, I learned as a child if you weren't perfect and did what was right, you were going to hell.

* *See bibliography*

I was taught I was born with original sin, and all the minor things I did wrong were venial sins and the big ones were the black mortal sins. So most of the time I felt completely unworthy to receive help from God. That made it even tougher for me to trust. I also turned the significant figures close to me, authority figures – my mother, father, priests and the nuns at school – into gods here on earth. Any bad thought or feeling I had toward them, was one more sin that thrust me into that black pit of hopelessness, powerless-ness, and helplessness.

Even after I got sober, I struggled mightily with self-reliance because I wasn't dealing with the cause of it. The conflict continued. There was always a part of me wanting to take risks, hell-bent for leather; and another part of me terrified – because those risks were way outside my comfort zone. And the AA slogan, "Let go and let God," just wasn't working for me.

I came to the realization that a lot of the decisions I made were made out of fear, not from strength. I wanted desperately to shift that pattern, to trust. But the path was rocky – one day I would let go, the next I would hold on – the conflict raged and my self-reliance ebbed and flowed.

I remember one particular day. We had been back on PEI for a year-and-a-half, spiraling downward financially. On this day I received a cheque for one week's worth of work; it was $120. When I picked up the mail, I found $285 worth of bills.

My typical way of handling that kind of helplessness or powerlessness was to fly into a rage, which my wife often witnessed. This time she said: "If you're going to act like an animal, get out with them." There was this beautiful spot in the woods I used as a retreat, with tall cedar trees and a brook snaking in and around them. It was January and very cold with lots of snow on the ground. I lay in the snow bank, fuming with rage; the snow around me slowly melting. I looked up at a maple tree, which had only one leaf left. That leaf was shaking back and forth, back and forth, in the wind. All of a sudden as I looked directly at it, the leaf let go and it floated gracefully down, zigzagging back and forth until it landed softly in the water and floated down the stream. It was like God saying through nature, "Donn, let go, let go." And for the first time in a long time, I felt that peace again, the peace of trusting and letting go. Self-reliance is a pale substitute for this powerful, all-encompassing, connected feeling.

The last time I had even thought about this internal peace was two months before I quit drinking. One day while working in Banff on the Rimrock Hotel, I was sitting on the edge of the concrete, looking down the canyon. Snow was softly falling, and you could see deer walking through the deep snow. I was thinking, my God, wouldn't it be nice to be as peaceful inside as nature is. I wanted to experience this incredible natural feeling of Oneness every day, all day.

If this seems like a dream to you, I understand. It did to me, too. But today, it is not a dream. Almost everyone I work with experiences this wonderful sense of Oneness, and once experienced, our system can keep retracing this connection, providing we encourage it. I compare Oneness to the water on this planet. Every body of water is connected in one way or another, through streams, lakes, oceans and precipitation. It is the same for us as human beings. In one way or another, we are all connected to each other and to every living thing, whether we realize it or not. When we have layers and layers of protection around us, like layers of cotton batting, we aren't aware of the connection, but it is always there.

The state of Oneness can be constant, but in the beginning we have to build up to it, just like building a muscle. In this state of Oneness there is a complete trusting and letting go, feeling one with the universe and everything in it. How that happens, though, is not as simple as it sounds. We have to dissolve the developed ego, which includes all the multitude of ways we convince ourselves that we are important, loved, safe or not safe. One of the goals of the developed ego can be to maintain the status quo, which it believes is safer than changing and moving into unfamiliar territory. The status quo is so familiar it often feels quite normal. I'd like to share an experience I had with my grandson as a way of explaining how powerful our minds are in creating our perceptions and our desire for the status quo.

Last spring, my 10-year-old grandson came for a visit from Prince Edward Island. I live in a house in West Vancouver with a rock stairway that glides all the way down to the ocean. The second morning Daniel came down to the ocean where I spend my two hours meditating and said: "Grampy, what do you do down here?"

I proceeded to explain some things to him. Just then he heard a loud noise in the bushes and got very scared. I described to Daniel how the way he saw his world created the meaning he gave to the loud noise – something scary. I got him to take a rock and throw it in the water. Then I said, notice the way the ripples flow out from the rock. Eventually, those ripples will come back to us. (In one of his books, Deepak Chopra talks about this effect at great length. He says our thoughts can be so solid you could dress them up and put clothes on them.) I told Daniel his thoughts would come back to him. If he chose to think in a very limiting, constricting way, for example that terrible things were going to happen – then he would notice if that happened. If he chose to think wonderful, beautiful thoughts, that's what he would notice flowing back to him.

I asked him how many channels on the radio he listens to at any one time. And of course, as a 10-year-old would, he said one! So I said, so how come you don't listen to two of them at the same time? He said because you can only hear one at a time. And I said, that is exactly how our thoughts work. Whatever way we choose to think, that is the station we are listening to and those are the thoughts that come back to us.

I also told him, simply, how his nervous system works and how his earlier experiences of getting scared created his perceptions. When Daniel was younger, he had been left alone with a doctor during laser surgery on a birthmark on his face. He became terrified and after that he was always on alert for being abandoned. I showed Daniel how to feel safe and strong, and he has been doing that ever since. Every weekend when I talk with him, he tells me how much progress he is making. His Mom reports that he hasn't had any scary experiences for almost a year; he previously had three or four a week. I can't help but think how wonderful it is, at his age, not to go through the pain and suffering that I did. We are not victims of our thoughts, perceptions and feelings. We can actually change them. Deepak Chopra states: "Perception appears to be automatic, but in fact it is learned… if you change your perception, you change the experience of your body and your world."* We are not meant to be self-reliant in a way that disconnects us from the world around us and we do not have to settle for the status quo. Daniel can grow up knowing he is connected to all the energy of life.

Let me ask you: When you are self-reliant, doing a task, activity, whatever – what feelings do you have? Do you feel connected to everyone and every-thing around you, or do you feel independent, alone, on your own? What does your body feel like? Is there a relaxed, easy-flowing feeling or is it one of tightness or readiness? How easily do you include others in what you are doing? These questions can help you understand the implications of self reliance. Self-reliance can be useful in some contexts but, as an overall perspective or way of living, it falls far short of what I feel is possible for all human beings.

JULIE IS ANOTHER CLIENT I WORKED WITH WHO KNEW A LOT about self-reliance and its devastating consequences. She was accepted into the law faculty at McGill at 19. She had huge ambitions: "I wanted to better myself." Law school was competitive and aggressive. Julie quickly realized she was in over her head, but she kept pushing herself. "They kept telling me what an honor it was to be there at my age. I was in, *among the favored few*." And she stayed with it because, as she puts it, "Only quitters quit; it was a terrible experience for me." She ended up with such poor grades, she couldn't get into a post-graduate program. "I felt I had no control of anything."

She started to lose weight. People noticed this and complimented her on her self-discipline. The attention replaced the status she had initially enjoyed at law school. So the weight kept coming off, until finally, Julie didn't

* See bibliography

have enough energy to count calories. She knew something had to change!

Her best friend was applying for flight attendant school with Air Canada and encouraged Julie to come along. It gave her an excuse to leave her experiences at McGill behind and get away from an unhealthy relationship. Air Canada gave Julie the chance to live some of her life-long dreams of travel and flexible hours. She became a responsible member of a crew, a team player. Julie really fit in but, eventually, she began to question whether this was as far as she would go, career-wise. So she sought out a career counselor. At the time Julie was in a relationship with Chris. Chris had done work with me and kept telling Julie to see me – not some career counselor. "It was Donn this, Donn that, I would roll my eyes and laugh."

Julie found that her 'career sessions' quickly evolved into a study of her past relationships. "I was going in to talk about my career and ended up talking about an old boyfriend." After a year with the counselor, Julie felt she was not making progress: "I was just retracing familiar ground." The psychologist would stroke her ego and she admits she liked that. But she started to realize that she would spend 45 minutes talking and then he would say, "I'm sorry Julie, we're out of time, I'm going to have to let you go now."

Julie and Chris's relationship was suffering. For the first time in her life, Julie was with someone who admitted he couldn't be her constant morale booster. "He said I love you, but I can't do this for you, you have to do it for yourself." Julie had to learn to be her own biggest fan. Until Chris, Julie gravitated towards men who were more than happy to control her. "I ended up with an eating disorder as a result of one relationship," she says, shaking her head. "Why was I always expecting someone else to fulfill my emotional needs? I'm glad I met Chris – he certainly put me on the right track about having to love myself first. We broke up, but we stayed in touch. He kept suggesting I meet Donn and I resisted until I realized that traditional counseling was doing nothing for me. Maybe, in order to move on and get what I wanted out of life, it was worth a try.

"I just felt I had so much more potential than I was aware of, but I couldn't get my engine started. I was scared – of failure. My experiences at law school deflated me and it was hard to trust my instincts."

As Julie remembers it, she flew to Vancouver and I met her at the airport. "He had a very warm smile, but he didn't cut me any slack! To every answer I gave him, he would ask: Why? I knew right then, this was going to be hard. That's not how it's supposed to go. My previous therapist was so sweet – he would just listen and tell me everything would be OK. But Donn was not doing that; he was getting right to the heart of the matter. Before I realized it, he was identifying patterns I was using, like one of my favorites: 'Worrying will solve everything.' I used to have cycles of insomnia because I worried so much. After that ride from the airport, I knew things were going to change for me."

Julie's first session left her drained; she said her head was spinning – "but I trusted Donn and his process and I tried to give as much of myself as I could." She had stored up so many feelings that when they finally came out, she says, "It was overwhelming. I bawled and bawled at that first session because I was letting go of so much." For Julie, the defining moment came at her second session, when she started to feel, for the first time in her life, unconditional love. It totally transformed her. "In the second session, I cried for joy. It was the best moment I've ever felt." I still remember Julie's face and her statement: **"My God, who turned on the lights to the universe around me?"**

Then September 11th happened.

Julie was on duty in New York, grounded at the airport in the aftermath of the destruction. The crews were evacuated and lost in the sea of people uprooted from their schedules and routines. "I knew my instincts were right on because I'd just gone through the Excelessence process." Julie remained strong and calm, keeping busy until it was safe to go home. Once there she let her feelings flow, releasing the emotions she felt: sadness, rage and confusion.

"I let it all out – then stepped outside on my balcony. Right then and there I had this epiphany. **I was the wind moving the leaves and the setting**

sun glinting on the river – and I started to cry. I realized this is what it's all about and I felt so connected and so grateful to be alive. I am not paralyzed with fear anymore; I don't let fear stop me. I can live each day to its fullest."

15

I see the universe as a whole and its simple principle of creation
as one unit, repeated over and over... as evidenced in
the universal heart-beat to which every pulsing thing in the
light-wave universe is geared to act as one unit of one whole.
WALTER RUSSELL

I HAVE BEEN TALKING ABOUT SELF-RELIANCE AND HOW IT WORKS against us. The alternative to self-reliance is *Oneness*. For me this was an easy jump to make but I now understand that, had I been educated in a more traditional way, I likely would have had a much harder time blending psychology and spirituality. Steve talks about his struggle with this issue:

Having a father who is a minister, one grandfather who was a missionary, and another grandfather who was a minister and dean at a seminary, I had no choice about attending church each Sunday. It was a duty, no questions asked. From that experience I developed a belief that it is wrong to force or coerce others into specific religious or spiritual beliefs. It was the proselytizing that I resisted and vowed not to do with others. In university, psychology and spirituality are kept quite separate and that suited me to a tee. What I didn't realize is this was an obstacle for me and, ultimately, for my clients.

In my personal journey, and this was reflected in my work with clients, my focus was on becoming self-responsible (more effective in handling things on my own) and no longer a victim to circumstances or symptoms. I hadn't taken the extra step of moving to connection with Spirit in the greater spiritual realm and never having to be on my own. This next step was a big shift in paradigm: not just from victim to self-reliance but to be connected with Spirit. In this third paradigm individuals are encouraged to stand in their True Power while connected to Spirit. This differs from how some religions conceive of it, there is no diminishing of self will or dissolving of self into the void. Donn's approach opens the door to the link between us and spirituality, separate from religion, and is a key part of the process of wholeness. When I observed the impact of this connection, the Oneness, I realized how I had boxed myself in with my own approach.

Steve formally encountered this concept of Oneness when I introduced him to the life of Walter Russell. I had read about Russell in Glenn Clark's book, *The Man Who Tapped the Secrets of the Universe.** I felt an immediate connection with what Russell was saying because I already knew about Oneness from my own experiences. In order to fully appreciate what Russell has to offer I feel it is important to give you a taste of his extraordinary life, as Glenn Clark described it.

Walter Russell was born in Boston, Massachusetts, in 1871 and died on his 92nd birthday, in 1963. At 85 he was more active than ever, looking to the years ahead as the most important years of his life. He lived and worked at Carnegie Hall in New York for many years. "A musician from infancy, he secured a position as church organist at 13 and entered art school. He has been entirely self-supporting and self-educated since then. Because of his versatility and love of doing many things at a time, he developed the feeling he had five lives within his one. Each life spanned from five to 20 years and

* See bibliography

168

was the transition for the next."

He used his music to finance his education in art; he taught music, played, composed and even conducted. In his transition to art he became an illustrator for books and magazines, an art editor and a war artist. In 1900 he completed an allegorical painting entitled *The Might of the Ages*, which toured museums in Europe winning honors in France, Belgium and Spain.

Next, Russell focused on portrait painting. He traveled across the country painting portraits of children, including the children of President Theodore Roosevelt. In 1914 he changed the subject of his portraits to adults, with equally notable results. He also wrote extensively and delivered hundreds of lectures.

Although he never studied architecture, he designed and built more than $20 million worth of buildings in New York City, among them the world-renowned Hotel des Artistes and the first Hotel Pierre on Park Avenue. He financed the building, sold all the stock, and pioneered the principle of cooperative ownership, previously deemed unsound, which became recognized as an economic principle throughout the world.

At 56 years of age, Russell made an abrupt transition to sculpture. With no formal training, he took on the commission for a sculpture of Thomas Edison when another artist dropped out. To understand the magnitude of this challenge, imagine a pianist suddenly taking up the violin for a concert at Carnegie Hall. He says: "It was very unwise for me to do, perhaps, because with such a great man as Edison as my subject, I might not have survived a failure. But I never let the thought of failure enter my mind." What he focused on, instead, was his belief in man's unlimited power. Rather than technical practice, he relied on "inspirational meditation."

Russell went on to complete many portrait busts of famous subjects. Early in his sculpting career, he was commissioned to prepare a monument to Mark Twain which consisted of 28 figures. The complexity of this task multiplies exponentially; the second figure was four times as difficult as the first. People called him a fool and fully expected him to fail – but the

Mark Twain monument was so successful that the British government commissioned a copy.

Walter Russell made his last transition into science and philosophy. He pioneered in work that foreshadowed two of the greatest discoveries of modern times: the isotopes of hydrogen, which led to the discovery of heavy water, and two new elements that were used in building the atomic bomb.

And what philosophy guided him in all this? Russell embraced many unusual concepts. For example: "I sincerely believe that every man has consummate genius within him. Some appear to have it more than others, only because they are aware of it more than others are. The awareness or unawareness of it is what makes each one of them masters – or holds them down in mediocrity. I believe 'mediocrity is self-inflicted and that genius is self-bestowed.'"

He didn't believe in fatigue and claimed he knew the secret to never tiring. "Joy and happiness are the indicators of balance in a human machine, just as a change in the familiar hum in a mechanism immediately indicates an abnormalcy to the practiced ear of the mechanic. An inner joyousness, amounting to ecstasy, is the normal condition of the genius mind. Any lack of that joyousness develops body-destroying toxins. You must love anything you must do. Do it not only cheerfully, but also lovingly, and the very best way you know how. That love of the work, which you must do anyway, will vitalize your body and keep you from fatigue."

He also believed that if you held to *knowing* that something good would happen, it would. As a teenager standing in line to buy symphony tickets, he realized he did not have enough money. But he believed that somehow it would come to him, and it did. A stranger asked if he would sell his place in line. He said no, but he offered to buy the tickets for this person and deliver them to his office. The man was delighted and instantly agreed. Observing this, others followed suit. By the time he reached the ticket booth he not only had enough money for his tickets, he had money left over.

I have seen this principle in action personally. My son Trevor works in Japan and wanted to come home for Christmas. The ticket was $990 and he only had $800. Like Walter, I encouraged him to believe he would get his ticket. One day $30 arrived, a repayment of a long-forgotten loan. Then he found a $100 bill in a wallet he hadn't used for months. Lastly, in checking an old bank account he discovered $60 – making an exact total of $990. Each time Trevor was tempted to give up, I encouraged him to "stay in line."

Russell's life intrigued me so much I wanted to know what he based his life perspective on. I learned that most important to him was the over-riding concept of *rhythmic balanced interchange* and our interconnectedness. So often in life, things seem complicated and yet Russell's message centered on the simplicity of the whole design of our existence. When I read this, it seemed to make total sense. Russell reports: "Thus I was made to see the universe as a whole and its simple principle of creation as one unit…as evidenced in the universal heart-beat to which every pulsing thing in the light wave universe is geared to act as ONE UNIT OF ONE WHOLE."

These words reverberated in my brain – *one unit of one whole, universal heart-beat, we are all interconnected.* The power and scope of the idea just kept flooding my brain. On the conscious level I could hardly comprehend the words: what did they really mean? – and yet inside I could feel the excitement welling to the surface. My mind went flying after the possibilities for our world if everyone realized they were indeed connected.

Aboard Apollo 14, the astronaut Dr. Edgar Mitchell experienced instant "global consciousness" when he viewed our planet from afar. He felt a profound sensation –" a sense of universal connectedness." This was such a powerful experience that when he returned to earth, he dedicated the next 30 years to helping people raise their consciousness and understand that we are all one. I was amazed by the striking similarity between Mitchell's awareness of connection, gained from his lunar experience in 1971, and Walter Russell's insight in 1921 when he was given the understanding of our interconnectedness.

I too was beginning to see the world as Russell described it. What is more important, I was convinced I could guide clients to this place of Oneness. I could assist them in reconnecting with what had always been inside and would now be part of their conscious awareness. Once we are reconnected to our core, the power that is released is amazing. **This is the step that reveals the extraordinary within each of us.**

JULIE DESCRIBED THE ONENESS AS BEING CONNECTED TO THE universal energy, when she said: "My God, who turned on the lights to the universe around me?" Each person experiences it differently, but there is no doubt people can access this state of being and sustain it, and when that happens, people can make changes that almost seem like magic. I found clients were getting the results they wanted, in less and less time.

I spent so many years trapped in pain and misery, then found a way out of the "pit." It is exhilarating to be able to help others liberate themselves. I am still amazed sometimes at how quickly this transformation can take place. When passion is released, it is beautiful. Passion for life is so special to me, that helping others connect with their passion is a joy I treasure.

16

It is a subtle shift from pushing ourselves
to be the best in the world,
to allowing ourselves to be the best for the world.

DEWITT JONES

"ORGANIZED, CONTROLLED, FOCUSED, DRIVEN, OUTGOING, enthusiastic, energetic. All these words describe me, Tina. I work hard in the demanding world of technology marketing but I have plenty of outside interests: music, dance, extreme sports. I consider myself to be very confident. Why would I need this process? I think I am a really stable and balanced person, and I wondered how much I could get from this program. On the other hand, I did feel pressure. I was always go, go, go, forcing myself to put that effort in. Raised with very high expectations, I had to be the best at everything – and was: straight-A student, piano practice an hour or two every day, dance classes six times a week. My family had very high standards and I had to hold myself to those standards.

"I was excited but nervous about taking the process. I had some skepticism: how do you really change a person's attitude or persona in two-and-a-half or three hours; how can that be? It's too quick. I was brought up to believe the more effort you put in, the more hours and dedication you have, the better the results."

Tina is talking about the thought virus: *No pain, no gain*. This virus can affect everything we do. Tina's whole way of approaching life was to work hard, put in the time and effort; only then do you deserve the rewards. On the surface this may look like a good model, that it's working, but Tina knew it was taking its toll. Actually, for many people high expectations can and do create immense pressure. This pressure can throw even elite performers off their game, because the striving tightens their system, preventing them from relaxing and reaching their true potential.

The more we force or push in trying to reach a goal, the more we actually become weaker and weaker. I read an article last spring, quoting Todd Bertuzzi of the Vancouver Canucks, that captures this perfectly. "We are so uptight, we are squeezing the paint off our hockey sticks." This is the pressure that is so destructive. When we let go and relax, the universe is able to flow through us. This comes through in many forms; enhanced performance, creativity, lightness and fun, to name a few. Tina was very familiar with the pressure to perform; she had lived with it all her life, and so had I.

"I was intrigued enough to work with Donn because I readily admit, I love self-help things and thought this was another one. I'd gone through the Tony Robbins tapes, so I was familiar with limiting beliefs and overcoming them. But nothing prepared me for how Donn would deal with my belief system. I worked with him one-on-one and the impact was immediate; there's no comparison to anything I had taken before. I was moved by the clear-cut approach Donn took to get right to the root of my conflicting values. I wanted to be the best – but I had all these negative thoughts, weak thoughts, holding me back. How could I be the best or put my best effort in, if negative thoughts are going through my mind?"

Tina is right on the money when she questions the effect negative thinking can have on our system. I often share a metaphor with clients to really lock this point in. Imagine you have a wonderful new Ferrari, and just before you take it for a fast drive, you put a spoonful of water in the gas tank. It is only a spoonful – what harm can such a small amount do? How many people would do such a thing? Yet we do this emotionally every day. We add a spoonful of doubt or a spoonful of fear and wonder why we don't perform at our best.

"Right after I finished the process, I was awash with amazement. I felt I was seeing everything more clearly. I felt so much more positive and I felt this huge sense of energy and clarity. This process brings you back to who you are. I feel there's a whole world out there, and there's nothing holding me back. I have everything within me to get out there and do everything I want.

"A funny thing happened after I took the program. I walked down the steps and I saw a piano in the hallway, I thought: wow, that's a beautiful piano! Donn said, 'Why don't you play something?' A few hours before, I know I would not have had the nerve to sit and play at such a spontaneous request. I would have been self-conscious, I would have been nervous, I might have played, but with a lot of angst. Now I just sat down and played. I was like, yeah, I haven't played in a while… I should play more often!

"I've become more me, without the crap that holds you back. I feel confident without the hidden nervousness and I have a really high level of energy, yet ironically, the people closest to me say I am much more relaxed.

"Then, some really coincidental things began happening. As soon as I finished the process, I went back to my office. I checked my voice mail; the library had called to say: 'We've found your daytimer.' I lost my daytimer three-and-a-half-years ago. I really regretted losing it because there were pictures in it, friends' addresses, thoughts and quotes I'd written down. Now suddenly, three-and-a-half years later, it appears. I don't pretend to understand things like this, but I do believe everything happens for a reason."

I believe it was no accident that Tina lost her daytimer in the first place. Something was going on at that time and the loss reflected it. When that issue was cleaned up in her system, her system rebalanced itself and abundance automatically flowed in to replace the loss. This concept of synchronicity may seem far-fetched, but I have witnessed it over and over with people I've worked with and I no longer question it. It is as simple as this: when you release constricting energy, expansive energy will automatically flow in. This basic principle has been clearly articulated by many people – Deepak Chopra, Caroline Myss, James Redfield – who readily share how they live this principle on a daily basis.

LIKE TINA, MARK IS ANOTHER REALLY TALENTED PERSON CAUGHT in the web of 'work harder'. Mark is a master homebuilder who values the country lifestyle so much he moved his corporate headquarters out to his property west of Calgary. While others head into the concrete jungle every morning, Mark's staff take the opposite direction down a gravel road to a rustic but high-tech building nestled among the spruce and poplar trees. Mark's commute is a gently sloping path from his front door to his office door. It would appear to an outsider he has found the ideal balance between life and work. But looks can be deceiving.

As a master craftsman Mark sought and demanded perfection every day, just the way I had when I was building high-rises. When asked for one word to describe himself, he said, "driven." And others agree with that, whole-heartedly. His best friend Dave, whom you will meet later, says Mark is never relaxed, even on vacation. The inability to relax may have made Mark a success in business, but it was slowly destroying him inside. He was always searching for a way to relieve the anxiety and stress. He admits that working harder was a way to keep his anxiety level in check. He read lots of books and tried several self-help programs, searching for answers. "Working lots, without much rest, seemed to complicate it more. I had extreme moments of anxiety, I couldn't relax, I had all this nervous energy. And I had panic attacks I didn't know how to combat."

Mark said he was willing to "try anything" but his big concerns were cost and my track record. Mark was extremely skeptical until we got started. One day he would call and say he was keeping the appointment, the next day he'd call and say he'd changed his mind. This went on for a full week. Finally, Mark made a commitment and we got started.

"After working with Donn, I felt very calm and relaxed, at peace. Ironically, I worried I was too calm and relaxed. 'How can I be this calm?' I wondered." He laughs about this now. For Mark the shift was immediate on all levels of his life, socially, at work, and with his family. "My wife noticed the change very quickly; she noticed I wasn't as hyper. At work I was able to carry on a conversation for more than 15 minutes without losing track or focus. It was quite a difference.

"I was known for my high energy, but I began to realize it was not good energy, it was driven energy. My new focus gave me all the positive energy I needed for my work without causing me emotional pain. My closest colleagues started asking me – what the hell have you done to yourself?"

Looking back over the past two years, Mark is very aware of how he changed. "For me, it was one of the best things I've done; it was a big change for me. I didn't tell many people about it, until much later. I wanted to make sure I could say, with full conviction, that it had really made a difference in my life. And I can say that now. Donn has made a huge difference for me.

"One other difference is the amount of work I was doing. When I met Donn I was building eight houses a year. This was a full schedule for me, and I was really struggling to keep up. The following year I built 15 houses with much less effort. **The ceiling of how high I could go just opened up.**"

When a "ceiling opens up" we are accessing more energy and this is about working with what I call *effortless effort*. Because there is no conflict in the system the effort feels so much easier, so much more natural. For Mark this translated into accomplishing more with less stress. For others it opens up the energy for healing or for performing with greater consistency. For me my creativity soared.

Dave had been watching all the changes. "Actually, I noticed a year before Mark said anything to me, the changes in him. Before, all he did was work. I think the personal side of his life wasn't as important to him. When

I saw him start to relax, take a family vacation, I knew something was up. Usually, he'd be away for two days and then be on a plane; you'd go to call him up and he'd be gone, checked out."

Dave should know what he's talking about; he and Mark have been buddies since high school. "We've been through a lot together. I'm not exactly an expert on Mark, but I am an expert on integrity. Mark is awesome. He waited a whole year to talk to me, till he knew the results were real. With this process it's hard to tell, it's so subtle; but the changes in him and his wife were huge. Also, Mark is not a guy to throw money away; when he made the decision for himself and his wife to take the process, I knew it was serious."

Dave continues, "I had no intention of following Mark's example, but I was intrigued when I had the chance to meet Donn. We played golf and spent the day getting to know each other. A couple of things Donn said caught my attention. Like, 'You can get rid of fear, you can let go of things instantly.' Donn asked if that would interest me, and I said absolutely, because I do have some fear and anxious moments."

On the surface, Dave is another person who looks like he has it all. He owns a golf course and is a housing developer. He's married to a wonderful woman and has two kids. His life is great. "My life has been good for a long time, but obviously it could be better. I'm the kind of guy who's at my peak when I've got four balls in the air, not one. I like to multitask, I would say I'm a quick thinker; I'm happiest and most fulfilled when I'm challenged. But with all this exciting challenge came anxious moments – I'd wake up in the middle of the night with tons of things going through my mind. My mind would be racing and I would be trying to put out fires that hadn't happened yet. I heard Donn say, 'There is one core problem; we can have 120 symptoms we're trying to deal with, but it's all from one core issue. And when we deal with that problem, it all shifts, and things change.'

"After Excelability, a lot of things are different for me. I accept things as they are, I sleep very soundly now; I'm not judging myself all the time and the feelings keep growing. I have a lot of peace in my life, more than ever before. I continue to enjoy my crazy schedule, but with less tension because I am focused in the now – where I am right at this moment.

"I also experienced positive changes in my relationships, mostly with my son. My wife and I are very close, we've got a really nice relationship, but my son and I – I would snap at him. That's changed. **I'm not nearly as stressed with him as I was, and I'm the one who's changed**. And the result is he's not fighting for my attention anymore. Lanny is 11 and now we're really close; we're tight. Doing Excelability was worth it just for that."

I agree with Dave. If we can make a difference for even one child, it's worth it all. Tapping into potential, whether it is a child's or an adult's, is like releasing energy into the whole world. Everyone benefits.

SPEAKING OF BENEFITS, WHAT ABOUT WORKING WITH SOMEONE who feels he hasn't used his full potential? Maybe most people feel this way but I was surprised to hear these thoughts from a very successful man like Mike.

Mike is a CEO of an international company. Even after enormous international success he felt he still hadn't reached his true potential. I remember Mike saying, "If you were to ask my wife, my boss, my employees, they would all agree that I have accomplished enough for a lifetime and have enjoyed tremendous success in my business life. I should be able to stop today and be satisfied with my business accomplishments. But I felt I had not yet tapped into my full-potential, meaning I had more to give which would allow for even greater accomplishments in my life".

Just the way Mike expressed this was all I needed to hear. I was instantly intrigued and told Mike: If it hasn't been tapped yet, I bet we can do it.

Whenever we are not living to our full potential it is because we have governors in our system. Earlier I mentioned how a car has a governor to prevent it from going too fast. Likewise, we have governors in our systems that stop us from reaching our full potential. In the world of sports, if an athlete has a slump, when they have been a consistently high performer, there's a governor in their system restricting them. Traditionally this "slump" would be linked to insecurity. In fact, if you look deeper, under the insecurity there is a deep-seated fear of "having it all."

Six months later Mike took the process. Mike sums it up succinctly: "As a result of taking the Excelability process, I went from experiencing my best performance one day out of seven, to realizing my best performance 75 per cent of the time. The remaining 25 per cent were not bad performance days, they were just something less than my standard for a best day." The changes Mike made are even more noteworthy because he was already at such a high level of performance.

Clearly people were making changes in their well-being, health and performance. Now, I wanted to return to my love of sports and refocus my energy in the world of athletics.

17

Life is either a daring adventure or nothing.
HELEN KELLER, 1880 – 1968

I BEGAN WORKING IN VANCOUVER IN JANUARY OF 2001, AND ONE
year later athletes I had assisted were in Nottingham, England, competing
in a world rowing regatta. It all began with an opportunity to work with the
women's rowing team at the University of British Columbia. I spoke with
their coach, Craig Pond, who had studied sports psychology in the past.
"Sure, I was skeptical – for 30 seconds," says Craig. "By the end of our initial
meeting, I couldn't wait to get the team into Donn's hands. Donn had
promised: Give me a crew and you will see a significant and measurable
improvement to their racing times." Craig set up a meeting for me with all
the rowers so they could decide for themselves.

At the meeting I asked for a volunteer to do a demonstration so they
could get a feel for how different my approach was and what they were
getting into. Amanda, the most senior rower, gamely came forward. In my
demonstration, I asked for her "best row" and her "worst row." This is like the

recipe for a cake; I want to know all the ingredients in a person's best and worst row. I ask really specific questions to understand the subtle and not so subtle differences between the two rows. Questions like: What does your future look like, is it clear or hazy? If there was a large clock on the wall, how fast or slow would the hands be moving? What are you saying to yourself – you know that voice that sometimes will not be quiet? These questions may seem unusual, but let me show you how they relate.

Using time as an example, a person perceives time quite differently when they are at their best and when they are not. Most people have had the experience of time flying by or moving at a snail's pace. The rate at which time is moving is actually not changing; only our perception of it is shifting. I ask the exact same questions for both the best and worst row and, in almost all cases, the two answers are as far apart as day to night. But these questions are just the starting point in helping athletes understand that their best and worst performances are no accident; they can be scientifically broken down into the essential elements.

I also use muscle testing as a way to demonstrate to people the differences, even physical differences, between their optimum performance and their worst. Most people think strength is stable; it doesn't change moment to moment. But muscle testing has proven this is not true. Our strength does change, depending on what is going on in our total system. Muscle testing comes from kinesiology.

KINESIOLOGY

Clinical research on the physiology of the nervous system and the holistic functioning of the human organism resulted in the 1970s in the development of the new science of kinesiology. This science, initially developed by Dr. George Goodheart, posited that the *mind* thinks with the body.

Our experience of events is expressed immediately through our body's reactions, leading to the effectiveness of muscle testing. When a person physically holds or thinks of a positive stimulus (healthy foods), a strong muscle response develops. This is what we would expect if the person's energy were flowing freely. But when we focus on a negative stimulus (white sugar, a cigarette), the muscles weaken noticeably. This makes sense if we imagine the person's energy being constricted. Research has taken the notion further, demonstrating that muscle testing can differentiate between life-threatening and life-enhancing stimuli, as well as between what is true and false. In fact, when subjects remembered times of anger, upset, jealousy, depression, guilt or fear, their muscles went weak. When remembering loving people or positive situations, their muscles were quite strong.

Research shows that our muscle strength reflects how our total system is functioning. When we are in alignment or at our best, our muscle strength reflects this. Likewise, when we are not at our best, it is reflected in our lack of muscle strength. The athletes found it hilarious to see how weak they were, when they were thinking about their worst row. When they concentrated on their best row, you could do chin-ups on their arm; with the worst, you could almost collapse the arm with one finger. They asked me to repeat the exercise just to be sure it wasn't a trick; and sure enough, the results were the same.

After the demonstration, when we asked for volunteers, hands shot up with enthusiasm. Twelve women were picked to participate in the process. Two days later we started. This was the first group of rowers I had worked with and I was curious to see what difference it would make, knowing nothing about the actual sport. In the past most of the athletic groups I'd worked with were in sports I knew and had played. My belief was that I didn't need to be an expert in the sport for the process to be effective. Time would tell.

Phase One of the process took two-and-a-half days. We started on Wednesday at noon and finished on Friday. The next day, in a competition, the rowers came very close to beating their top rival – a team they hadn't been able to beat over the past seven years. One month later, they did beat this team. The women were overjoyed at how powerful the experience was and how quickly they were seeing results. They were very eager to begin Phase Two, 10 days later.

Why 10 days? We have found, if a person is going to reverse their results, they will do it by the tenth day and, sure enough, some of them did. Initial results are exciting and encouraging, but what is much more important to us is long-term results. We want to be sure the person doesn't reverse the results over time and – if they do, we want to know the reason why. Often, this second phase of the process is more powerful and profound for people, because the changes take hold at an even deeper level. This is where the key to the safe is hidden, so to speak. This certainly was true for the rowers and, after the follow-up, their performance just kept getting better and better.

With the results the women were getting it seemed like a good time to interview them for the record, and I knew just the person to do it. Sherry Shaw-Froggatt, a freelance writer for magazines and newspapers, had already done an interview on the process and was thrilled to document more results:

Donn and I are sitting in a funky café (they're all funky in Vancouver) waiting to meet the women from the UBC rowing team. After an early morning workout on the water, they arrived several at a time, all smiles and laughter, greeting Donn like a favorite, revered teacher. I instantly sensed the team spirit among these vibrant young women. I am introduced to Amanda, Erica, Martha, Lindsay, Christina, Kathleen and Kitt. Lindsay's energy strikes me instantly.

The women were eager to share the changes they noticed in themselves and each other. Kitt jumps in first, "We had our best race performance ever, two days after the process." And Lindsay: "Going through the process was an emotional experience, especially to share as a group. Now we all have an understanding of how each other thinks. When someone gets frustrated we have a better understanding of why and how to help." Amanda follows this train of thought, "When something goes wrong, I now ask myself why? Why am I upset? Why is this affecting me? What do I need to do to change it and move on?" She pauses and then laughs, "It seems so simple now. When a problem arises, we sit there and sort it out; five minutes later we've cleared it and moved on!"

So why is that so different? "I used to get really pissed off and hold it inside for so long," Amanda admits. Kitt adds, "All that negativity just used to make things worse – personally and when we were rowing." "I learned how hard I was on myself," says Lindsay. "I was trying too hard to make things work – I learned to relax, step back and analyze why I'm feeling that way and within seconds, you change and get back on track." Kitt agrees: "I realized how critical I was of myself and now I see that the only person who matters in my life is me. I place less weight on what other people think. I take criticism better – I don't let it affect my emotional well-being."

So what have others noticed outside the team? "Apparently, the men's team had a pretty good laugh when they heard about our efforts. They were saying – go ahead, cry and blather – it's not going to make you row faster. Then we went out on race day and kicked butt. And the men's team got thumped! Suddenly the guys were paying attention.

"A lot of people have noticed how much happier we are, especially after a race or practice. When we get off the water, we know we've improved. We're not focusing on the negative. We are getting closer to winning all the time."

I asked the coach about the competitive factor. When athletes make peace with themselves, does it make them less of a competitor? Surprisingly not, he said! "The women are actually more competitive with each other now, but they are also gracious with each other – not getting angry when they lose. They encourage and compliment one another and, as a result, the team is united when it is time to race against other teams."

Craig says his job is so much easier now as a coach. There are no hang-ups in the boats. "I don't have to chew through all the emotional stuff." "It's like we enter the boats as true performers now," Martha explains, "no personality clashes, no worrying about why I didn't get paired with so and so." And Donn adds: This is what I keep telling coaches – the process cleans up the emotional blocks and leaves the coach free to work on the technical aspects of the sport.

Craig, for one, is relieved: "I want to focus on producing winning teams." I ask Craig if he's noticed any changes in the way the women process new skills or changes in training. "Way faster – they appear to be adapting instantly to anything new I show them; there is a willingness to accept change. There is zero negative energy in the boat. The feedback is instantaneous – they row faster and it's easier for me to do my job."

Craig adds, "It's all about eight people believing in one thing. A rowing shell goes really fast if all the people in the shell are doing the exact same thing, all of the time. When all eight people believe they can do that, the boat is going to be successful."

Donn asks the group: What about injuries, any changes there?

Lindsay jumps right in. "**When I get injured now I know it's not about anything physical. It's mental and I can feel myself** doing it to myself, so it's been really valuable to see this and correct it quicker." Craig agrees with Lindsay. "I've seen Lindsay suffer through injuries longer than anyone and so much of it was psychological. A good example of how she has changed happened a few weeks ago. She fell and hit the knee she had surgery on and she showed up the next day with no pain. I know for a fact that if this had happened a year ago, it would have been sore for days. She's bouncing back so much quicker."

Kit sums it up: "Donn can bring out what is innate in all of us – in such a gentle, effective way. It appears so simple in retrospect but to get there is the gift Donn gives you. Now we can take the steps ourselves and quickly get back on track with our lives. We're feeling this overwhelming confidence. I know I can row well and I'm feeling great."

Being in sync is the key. In rowing, if one person is off, it throws the whole team off. Rowers sit very close together in the boat and all the oars need to work in harmony. In a boat with eight rowers, if one person is out of sync, it's like a spider with broken legs, oars going in all directions. Working in unison is part of any team sport, but in rowing, the feedback is instantaneous. After the process everyone was in sync and contributed to the maximum of their ability. Once they were aligned internally, they automatically were aligned with each other externally. Even though there were eight individual athletes, they rowed as one.

From a coaching perspective, Craig found it effortless to correct technique and appreciated how little work was required on motivation because each athlete had their own internal motivation fully mobilized. The most impressive thing about the internal clearing is it not only enhanced their rowing, it made a significant improvement in their study patterns, test results, and relationships with all those around them.

All this preparation was leading up to the 120th Royal Canadian Henley Regatta in Ontario, the largest international club regatta in the world, with more than 2,600 athletes competing in over 1,700 events. In preparing for competition, athletes measure their performance against what is called the Gold Standard. These statistics are based on how close a team's time trials compare to what it would take to win a gold medal at the Olympics. Normally, a two per cent increase per season would be considered very good improvement. In five months, less than a full season, the scores jumped more than six per cent. The women's 'eight' went from 85 to 91 per cent, and the pairs went from 86 to 93 per cent. The athletes were very happy with their performance at the Royal Henley; they beat teams they had never been able to beat before. All in all, a very good year.

Working with the women rowers led to my working with the men's rowing team. But before I worked with the men I worked with their coach. Over the years I've worked with many coaches for hockey players, Olympic swimmers, golfers, etc. I know how pivotal the coach is. If the coach and the team are in alignment, the sky is the limit. After seeing the results with the women, Craig was really keen to take the process personally. He and Mike Pearce, head coach of the men's team, decided to do the process together. I was very pleased they were so open.

So what difference did it make for an already skilled coach? A very powerful piece of feedback came from Rob, a gold medal winner. "Mike was my coach for the previous two years and he always had a strong mental aspect to the game, telling us what we could accomplish for the year. Even though the words were the same this year, I could feel the difference. It was as if he truly knew what he was saying was going to happen, not just hoping it would. As a result of his overwhelming confidence, I knew and the whole team knew this year was going to be very different." And different it was!

The men's team were readying for the Commonwealth Games in England followed by the World University Championships a week later. As the competition loomed closer, I offered to work with the team so, mentally, they would be as strong as they were technically. In three days they would leave for the two world competitions.

I spent four-and-a-half hours with the team and my first

question was, "Did you have your best row this morning?" As luck would have it, they didn't. When I asked why, all nine men stood there in confusion, searching for an answer. Every answer they gave me was external: the equipment wasn't right, the water was rough, they woke up late, didn't eat their normal breakfast. They were further confused because I wouldn't let them get away with any of those answers. I was probing for answers that reflected what was going on inside the rowers, not problems with the environment or their technique. Slowly, I could see the lights come on. They started getting curious about how they could turn on their best performance at will. When we concentrated on the strategy for their best row and eliminated the contamination that created their worst row, they were pumped!

The team left two days later and, as Rob said, things sure were different. Even before they left, one boat was at a big disadvantage. The men's eight had two lightweights on the team rowing in a heavyweight division. At this level of competition this variable is enormous. Once they got to England more challenges arose. There were serious equipment problems, and for two days the rowers assembled and reassembled parts, trying to create working racing shells. While this was happening, crew members missed the scheduled meals and went without food. It was down to the wire! It was the day before competition, that the racing shells were finally patched together.

Nobody expected any medals from this team, but their confidence was unshakeable. At the Commonwealth Games, against all odds, they won a combination of two gold and two silver medals. The next weekend they won the gold medal at the World University Championships, beating the second-place team by a significant margin of eight seconds. This was truly an incredible accomplishment. There were many rowing victories in the summer of 2002, and as coach Mike Pearce said: "This past summer can go down in the history books as one of the most significant in over 80 years of rowing at the University of British Columbia."

18

Every day people are straying away from the church
and going back to God.
LENNY BRUCE, 1923 – 1966

ESSENTIAL TO UNDERSTANDING THE PROCESSES I HAVE DEVELOPED is my way of thinking about spirituality. To consider that such dramatic changes are possible for people, so quickly, requires something beyond human capabilities. To this end, I share my personal spiritual journey and the beliefs and knowing I have come to realize. These combine to form a foundation for the transformation process that has evolved over 23 years.

Ironically, to get to where I am today, closer to God/Spirit, required giving up everything I learned about God as a child. The path I followed spiritually has in many ways paralleled my search for professional skills. In my early upbringing, the Roman Catholic religion was central. We went to church regularly, once a week, and observed all church holy days with confessions every two weeks – and don't forget the 40 days of Lent and the rosary every day after dinner.

The religion of my childhood presented me with an image of God that was cold, stern, strict, authoritative, punishing, rigid and ultimately distant. I know this isn't how it is supposed to be, but this was how I experienced it at home through my parents, at school through the nuns or in church through the priest.

I grew up feeling bad, wrong and a sinner. In contrast, my initial experience of feeling pure and light was when I went to my first confession to be absolved of my sins. Connecting with the feeling of complete inner peace seemed to lie completely outside of me. I had no way to maintain this feeling except through the religious rituals I was taught and that only happened once. I didn't know the feeling came from being aware of my connection to God and being disconnected from all the constricting emotions and beliefs in the world around me. These feelings just kind of happened to me; they didn't seem to be something I had control over. In some ways this is no different from athletes' feeling powerless, while they wait for their best game to come back.

You will recall my journey to sobriety helped me begin the transition from an impersonal God to a personal God. For the first time in my life I started to have a real relationship with the God of my understanding. I was slowly moving away from feeling unworthy, a lowly creature trying to live up to what I thought were God's expectations of me. Rather, I was beginning to shift away from identifying who I was in terms of what I did, to understanding my worth lay in who I was, the core of which never changes.

I reached a significant milestone spiritually when I finished my fifth step in AA. Once again I felt whole and pure. I was beginning to glimpse the true power within; I was cleaning out all the past. But I didn't know what was creating the contamination, so I didn't know how to prevent it from recurring. It is one thing to clean up an oil spill like the Valdez; it is a completely different matter to figure out what went wrong, to prevent it from happening again.

Choice Theory further supported the direction I was already taking –

that we are internally motivated, not externally motivated, that nothing outside ourselves determines our behavior. The choice is internal. This fit the relationship I was now developing with God. It wasn't a relationship based on my trying to please or trying to be perfect in order to avoid punishment. Instead, it was more of what I was beginning to understand as unconditional love.

Because I had very little unconditional love in my life, I often felt alone. This aloneness was contaminated by my self-reliant attitude: I can manage on my own. As I have said, self-reliance has two sides, one of victim the other, independence. It doesn't matter which side you favor, it's still an unhealthy form of coping. This had nothing to do with God and everything to do with how I was viewing myself as separate from God. Fortunately, even though I felt that separateness, it wasn't a separation. It was only a perception. Looking back, especially on experiences where I easily could have died, I realized I had no control. I was being led, guided and taken care of. I was collecting lessons that would eventually teach me that control is an illusion. Control – the notion that if only we hold on for dear life and control everybody and everything around us, we will be safe. The question is – safe from what?

Notwithstanding this self-reliance, I still made it a point to meditate daily, first thing in the morning. No matter where I lived, I always found a sanctuary of quiet and stillness for meditation. I recall when I was working on the 18-story high-rise in downtown Calgary, how often I would get flustered, frustrated and overwhelmed. I would go to a small park across from the site with running water and trees, and find respite from all the chaos, confusion and pressure.

The biggest, single contribution to my development came from spending one to two hours a day for 23 years, in a quiet meditative state. There were many times I would not be able to stop my mind from racing, but I would stay there anyway. I drew on the richness of the quiet and tapped into a way of thinking and being that went way beyond me. Perhaps I took my cue from reading about Einstein, who pictured himself riding on the end of a light beam, or Michelangelo, picturing what David looked like in a block of marble, or Beethoven, as he wrote his fifth symphony.

I remember listening to Paul McCartney being interviewed about the song *Let It Be*. He woke up one morning after dreaming about the music, got out of bed, went to his piano and wrote down the music. Later he asked the other Beatles about the music, had they heard this song before? And they said no. He went to the studio and asked: had anyone there heard it? They all said no. That was when he realized it was original and two weeks later, he had written the lyrics to go with the music.

Most times when I am meditating, I am able to tap into this source of creative energy. As I was building a personal relationship with God, I began to have regular conversations with Him on just about any topic, including the odd argument that, needless to say, I lost. Like all of my relationships, this one was honest, casual, laid back, filled with humor and telling it like it is. To this day some people are quite startled at the frank conversations I have with God.

As a result of Dr. John Veltheim's lectures, and the personal talks we had, I made significant strides in understanding the difference between knowing and believing and my own sense of *knowingness*. I had thought believing was the ultimate; now I knew there was something much deeper and of much greater value. The challenge was finding the path to this knowing on a consistent basis.

The next rung on the ladder of my spiritual evolution was being introduced to Walter Russell, through Glenn Clark's book. In it, Russell talks specifically about Oneness – that each and every one of us is energetically linked and so we are linked to every living thing, including a universal power. When I read about his concept of Oneness, I experienced an immediate expansion of my awareness, a knowing that I was connected to everything in the universe. This experience of Oneness was very similar to my early experiences of lightness and peace. The biggest difference was this Oneness could be permanent, based totally on my inner essence, not on something that required a ritual or confession to reach. I have written a lot about this Oneness, not just because of its life-enhancing qualities, but because I believe it is essential to our very survival as human beings and as a species on the planet earth.

Deepak Chopra writes eloquently about what happens when people do not feel a sense of Oneness and connection. He states, "Seeing ourselves as separate, we create chaos and disorder between ourselves and things 'out there.' We war with other people and destroy the environment. Death, the final stage of separation, looms as a fearsome unknown; the very prospect of change, which is part of life, creates untold dread because it connotes loss. Fear inevitably brings violence in its wake. Being separate from other people, things and events, we want to force them to be what we want. In harmony there is no violence. Instead of futilely trying to control the uncontrollable, a person in unity learns acceptance, not because he has to but because there actually is peace and orderliness in himself and his extended body."*

I had been searching for Oneness for myself and others, but its impact goes far beyond the individual. It is also the answer for harmony on a global level. These ideas are not new or mine alone. Many people have expressed them over time. What I believe has not been available is a pathway to this Oneness that goes beyond awareness at an intellectual level. An actual process of **how** to achieve this, that doesn't take years. I am not talking about a perspective on life or a philosophy at an intellectual level, but a tangible experience that connects people with a deep knowing.

With this knowing, people report an immediate change in perspective as a result of the process I have developed. But it isn't a matter of thinking differently, or trying to be positive, it is an experience of being transformed, and shifting perception to a greater sense of connection with all of life. This effortless shifting of perspective, from what's wrong to what is possible, from fear to trust, and from loneliness to connection, is a key element of what is unique about this process. What I was developing was an actual

See bibliography

road map to guide others to this place of Oneness – a journey that would take hours rather than years.

The next quantum leap in my spiritual journey came immediately following my Crystal Mastery training. I was interested in the connection between our cells, as basic building blocks, our physical being, and higher states of consciousness. The link between these was the crystal lining of our cells. My meditation was taking me into areas of new discovery, but in Crystal Mastery training I discovered that my *developed ego*, my need for control, was still alive and well. I realized that whenever I felt disconnected, there was fear, the feeling of aloneness and having to manage things on my own. This is the polar opposite of the trusting that goes hand in hand with Oneness and connection. To one degree or another, this is the Jekyll and Hyde in each of us.

In Crystal Mastery training I dissolved a thick layer of my developed ego and added to my understanding of how to help others do the same. Again I saw the alchemy of three elements coming together – dissolving the developed ego, connecting with the universal power and linking this with my purpose in life – all leading to greater effectiveness in working with others.

If you think of a very large power plant, like the Hoover Dam, there is plenty of power there, more than one person could ever use. If a person is unaware that it exists or refuses to use this power, then for that person, it does not exist. If a person is aware it exists, but feels unworthy to use it, then the power is still unavailable for them. And what about the connection? If you use a thin power cord, or the cord is corroded, you will only receive low voltage. Many people think the problem is the source. The problem is **never** the power source; it's **always** our lack of awareness, willingness or diminished capacity to tap into its potential.

Once we are aware of our connection to this universal power, in a full and unrestricted manner, the challenge becomes how to keep it. For most of my life, whenever I got something I really wanted, I clutched onto it with such force that I created a binding constriction; the energy couldn't flow.

I needed to do the opposite, to connect gently, to be open to the pure joy within, allowing it to flow freely, trusting it will never run out and staying connected, knowing we are the co-creators of our lives.

19

We all need to be healed in the highest sense by making
ourselves perfect in mind, body and spirit.
The first step is to realize that this is even possible.

DEEPAK CHOPRA

AS I WRITE THIS, THE YEAR 2003 IS COMING TO A CLOSE. IT HAS
been a year of genuine growth. But the story would not be complete without
telling you about our research. We are currently pursuing three areas of
research: cancer, spinal injuries and Parkinson's disease. This research
provides an opportunity for discovery. I know the human body is an amazing
system and I feel privileged to have the chance to explore these new frontiers.
It's an exploration that's just beginning. Here are two examples of the
progress we have already seen in the areas of Parkinson's and cancer.

Parkinson's disease is certainly not something you would think has
an emotional component. It is generally viewed as a neurological illness,
which is irreversible. I had no personal experience with it, but once my
curiosity was piqued, it was hard to ignore. It was almost like: "OK, Donn,
if you believe in all this energy blockage stuff, let's see if it has any effect on
this illness." Knowing the symptoms were not my concern, it became an

interesting challenge to see if energy blocks were influencing the advance of the disease.

I met Mona in the spring of 2001, when her daughter Lynn, my colleague and the co-author of this book, asked if I would meet her. At 79, Mona had been struggling for 11 years with the gradually increasing and frustrating effects of Parkinson's. I said: Lynn, I have never worked with Parkinson's patients and, besides, the person has to be ready. We had learned through experience not to work with anyone unless they were ready. I was also thinking: She's too old, she won't be open to the concepts and ideas I have, which are very different from traditional approaches. Boy, was I wrong!

Lynn said: "I think she is ready"– and much to my surprise, she was right. When I asked Mona, "Do you think it is possible that psychological factors may be contributing to your illness?" She said, "Yes, it's possible and I'm game to find out what they are." It was her beautiful enthusiasm that convinced me; I enjoyed working with Mona from that day forward.

As we chatted I was looking for patterns in how she was dealing with life. I quickly became aware that Mona was using a strategy I refer to as "ignoring the oil light." It was very clear there were lots of signals that Mona had been ignoring. Just like the oil light on the dash, if you cover it up, you haven't removed the problem; you just don't see the light.

In the first session, when we were exploring events in Mona's life, she reached a point where her hand and body started shaking excessively. This was the signal I was looking for. It is the "conflict impasse," where the nervous system responds in a constricted manner and it almost always occurs out of the person's conscious awareness. As soon as Mona moved through this impasse, her hand and body quit shaking. It was clear that the shaking was directly linked to an emotional factor woven into her neurological wiring.

Mona was able to uncover significant events that constricted her energy, revealing patterns that eventually manifested themselves in her body. When shifts occur at the nervous system level, some results are immediate. Shortly after the first session, Mona was able to sit down and write easily, a task that had been very difficult before. Then Mona forgot to take one of her medications. This doesn't sound very significant – unless you understand Parkinson's; your body simply doesn't let you forget that you need medication. Mona breezed through a whole night, then the next day remembered this medication.

I viewed Mona's progress as moving along a continuum with the following possible stages:

Stage 1. Improved quality of life on current medication

Stage 2. Reduction of the "frequency of increase" in medication

Stage 3. No further increase of medication to maintain her current level of functioning

Stage 4. Decrease in medication, indicating greater dopamine production by her cells

Stage 5. Regeneration of brain cells sufficient to produce normal dopamine levels

A common side-effect of Parkinson's, related to the diminishing supply of dopamine, is depression. It can significantly decrease the feeling of well-being and quality of life. In Stage 1, there was a noticeable improvement in this area for Mona. She recognized a significant change in how she was feeling: "Even my children have noticed a difference. I'm willing to do more and go places at the drop of a hat." Taking medication requires a schedule and very careful monitoring. In his own story*, Michael J. Fox tells how he choreographed his whole day so his "good periods" would coincide with the activities he wanted to do; it was his main focus. In contrast, Mona was managing her medication as a minor scheduling matter. Surprisingly, even her golf game had improved. She was hitting that long ball further than ever. At 79 this isn't the way it is supposed to work, or is it?

Stage 2 addresses the rate at which medication is increased. Mona noticed a reduction in how often she was increasing her medication. This is significant because it is well-documented that a medication "ceiling"

*See bibliography

exists. Once you reach this ceiling, the medication loses its effectiveness. This is a frightening event because there are very few alternatives to medication. The slower you increase the medication, the more time you buy for new scientific advances to be made.

Mona is currently straddling Stages 3 and 4. She is on a quest to discover what will allow her body to produce more of its own dopamine naturally and allow her to reduce her medication. Up until now, no one has been able to stimulate new cells to start producing dopamine naturally. Once the dopamine-producing cells die, the body does not seem to replace them and the lack of dopamine is devastating to the nervous system. Reversing this pattern and encouraging new cells to produce dopamine would mean a breakthrough for all Parkinson's patients.

"I learned to listen to myself; only what I think matters. I never knew I was being so hard on myself." A lifetime of experiences brought Mona to this point. At 79 she is willing to explore new options and considers herself courageous. She quite calmly admits she wants to be the first person to beat Parkinson's.

IN NOVEMBER OF 2001, TONE WAS DIAGNOSED WITH STAGE 4 malignant melanoma, which is commonly considered to be terminal cancer. There were grave doubts about whether the scheduled chemotherapy he was scheduled to undergo would be effective.

Tone recalls "I checked into the cancer agency on Christmas Eve to start my chemotherapy. I was hooked up to IVs, getting hydrated, when the supervising oncologist came in and asked if anyone had talked to me about the procedure and what the outcomes were. Actually, nobody had; they had just told me to go in and get chemotherapy. She explained that, with tumors in my lung, my brain and a number of other areas in my body, the chemotherapy I was about to take was 'iffy.' There were questions as to whether it would work on my soft tissue tumors, and even if it did, it wouldn't work on my brain tumors. My brain tumors were so severe, she continued, I probably had only weeks to live. She suggested I go home and be with my family. So we unhooked and I went home for Christmas.

"I started with the traditional therapies, gamma knife [brain surgery] and chemotherapy, to give myself some time, to buy time. Then I pursued this alternative, Excelessence, which proved to be my salvation."

Tone agreed to an interview about his condition and his experience of working with Steve Davis:

I think for a lot of people, there are questions, doubts about whether something can really help them. Would you comment on that, what are your thoughts?

Well, I don't think it really matters what you are doing with your health – whether it means going to your doctors or a naturopath, going to a chiropractor, going to some spiritual center, there is always the question at the deep level: will this really help me? It's really about, do I have the courage to pursue what I believe? And with Excelessence, my quest for health and well-being was painless.

Painless in contrast to what?

Chemotherapy. I will give you my own experience: I couldn't eat for 42 days, I lost 40 pounds. I could hardly drink a glass of water. My skin burnt right off. I had neurotoxin damage to my nerves, I itched so badly that I was crazy with it, and the only thing that could really resolve that was painkillers. I just felt dreadful; my children were very afraid that I was actually dying from the chemotherapy. They couldn't understand why I was going away for treatment and coming back looking like hell.

After I completed my chemotherapy, I had a couple of motor vehicle accidents. I started to think, maybe I was supposed to die. The motor vehicle accidents sort of got me in a place of fear about death and about external things around death. Then I read a wonderful book written by an incredible woman who's an oncologist in the United States. In one of the chapters she mentions a patient of hers who was doing really well and then got some negative information from her physician and died. When I read that, I actually went into a big place of fear. All of a sudden, I doubted myself and my ability to survive. When I began to work with Steve Davis, we spoke about this, and he really helped me through that process of self-doubt.

What shifted in regard to those fears and doubts – because they were pretty deep seated?

Well in my most severe struggle with chemotherapy, especially when I was really under the gun and feeling very, very ill, I never gave up. I always knew that somehow I was going to get through this and it was my belief, I think, that got me through. I was starting to get much better and then, when the accidents occurred, and I read that book, all of a sudden I started doubting my belief system. I became afraid I wouldn't make it through this. I could feel my own life force diminishing, getting very dark and small. When I experienced Excelessence, I made such an important shift that I was able to go back to my beliefs and continue my process of getting better.

Tone, what part do you feel Excelessence played in your healing?

One of the most important aspects of Excelessence was an understanding of some of my root perceptions of myself and how these perceptions play out in our lives, including disease. I think doubts are very firmly implanted, entrenched in our own psyche and in our cells in our body.

The most important aspect for me was when I was in a place of self-doubt, I was able to work through that and start believing in myself, which is ultimately the way that I got better. Self-healing, but with external prompting.

You said you got back to that core sense of yourself and the doubts were gone. What did that feel like? Can you articulate what that felt like?

It's a very grounding kind of thing, a solid thing, which replaces a false sense of who you are, where beliefs are more in the head and more theoretical.

Excelessence was so important because I was able to make a shift and get back to my core beliefs, and continue my process of getting better. Physically, what really stands out in my mind is what happened to the tumors left over from the chemotherapy. They were still tender and sore and after Excelessence one of them very specifically shrank about a third. And that was in two weeks! I have to say, once I experienced that, I started to get pretty excited about the whole process. Not only did the size of the tumor change, but also the pain associated with it. The pain diminished considerably.

On August 30, 2002, when Tone went for his checkup, the doctors suggested he start coming back at three-month intervals. As Tone says, anybody who has ever had cancer realizes that when you go from weekly to monthly visits, that's a big step, but when you go from monthly to quarterly – that's a huge step in terms of your progress. You know the concerns and risks have dropped way down. Tone says: **Today I feel more alive than I ever have.**

Tone latest update is even more heartwarming. In August of 2003 he went to the United States to be evaluated as a candidate in a clinical trial involving a new "genetic delivery system" of treatment to combat melanoma. Melanoma is a very aggressive form of cancer and relapse is considered "probable." Even the gamma knife surgery that was used on his brain tumors often only lasts a short while and then the tumors return. So even when there is improvement the doctors follow a patient very closely.

Tone has always been very active in seeking out the newest research in cancer treatment. In order to participate in a trial a patient must fit certain criteria. Tone was shocked to discover he didn't qualify. First of all, they told him his immune system was handling things so well that the doctors commented, "whatever your immune system is doing is what we are really searching for." Secondly, to evaluate the effectiveness of the treatment they would need a tumor to biopsy after the treatment and Tone did not have any that were active. He only had old tumors that were no longer growing, which his body appeared to be slowly releasing. Tone is currently the longest-surviving melanoma patient his doctor has met, in his 30-plus years of medical practice.

Besides the results Tone achieved, and the hope that offers for others, one of the highlights for me is that Steve Davis worked with Tone. This book may be my story, but my vision goes far beyond that. Having colleagues work with me and duplicate my work is like giving birth and seeing your child take their place out in the world. What miracles can be achieved as we all continue to work together I can only imagine. Like in John Lennon's song *Imagine*, "You may say I'm a dreamer, but I'm not the only one, I hope some day you'll join us, And the world will live as one."

If we have no peace, it is because we have forgotten
that we belong to each other.
MOTHER THERESA, 1910 – 1997

THIS BOOK IS CALLED THE EXTRAORDINARY WITHIN AND I HOPE
you can see how this title came to be. I have shared my journey and the
journey of my colleagues in hopes that each person who reads this book
will be inspired to look within and to reach for the stars. To me it is extraordinary that a man raised in poverty, surrounded by addictions and fear
should find his way out of all that and have something to offer others.

In my twenties and thirties I would never have dreamed that I would
be offering guidance to others. I was so out of control in my own life that
to imagine guiding someone else would have terrified me. Yet inside lived
a dream; a dream to make a difference in the world. As I traveled down this
road, opportunities emerged and possibilities unfolded. I discovered what
I had learned from helping myself really did help others. I was able to teach
other people what I knew and, suddenly, I was not alone in my dream but
part of a team. As a team so many more things were possible. Excelanation,

our company, has a very big vision and it will take the joining of many hands to see that vision fulfilled. Reaching out to you the reader is part of achieving this dream and so is our training program developed by Steve Davis and Lynn Sumida. This program trains others in the skills we have developed so the impact expands exponentially.

We recognize our planet is in serious trouble. Just looking at pollution and the rate at which the earth is deteriorating, it is clear we must act together quickly to start reversing this. Many people feel the task is just too big and the time too short. If we think about this from our track record to date, and our seeming inability to work together, the picture does look quite bleak. But if we focus on changing our consciousness, rather than our actions, we open the door to great possibilities. **The potential we each have that is unused is the greatest waste of natural resources on the planet!**

Dr. Hawkins, in his book *Power versus Force,* believes that raising our consciousness is the only way to move ahead. I agree, and I know we now have the tools to do this. **From his research he has been able to predict the impact of consciousness.** He states if one person raises their consciousness to the level of 700, out of a maximum of 1,000 points, that single person can positively influence 70 million people. **If he is even close to right**, global change becomes much more feasible. But to attain such high levels of consciousness, we must release all the constrictions in our system. If we don't fully release the constrictions, we will waste a great deal of energy, constantly torn between feeling hopeless and trying to do more. James Redfield in his books *Celestine Prophecy**, *The Tenth Insight** and *The Secret of Shambala** beautifully articulates constrictions in action. Over and over, the characters in his book are consumed by doubt, anger and fear. Conversely, I think everyone knows what it is like to be around someone who radiates warmth, joy and well-being. You are rejuvenated just by being in their presence. According to Hawkins this is not in our imagination, it really is happening. Imagine if each of us was like that – radiating joy.

* See bibliography

As we look at the global situation I am reminded of something Virginia Satir, the famous family therapist, said: "The problem is never the problem, the coping is the problem." If she is right, what does this mean? It means that the environment isn't the problem and famine isn't the problem and disease isn't the problem. It is the way we are coping with these issues that is the problem. If we take this a step further, perhaps the way we are coping with each other is the problem. And ultimately it is the way we are coping with ourselves that is the problem.

Author Steven Covey in his book *Principle Centered Leadership* recommends: "If you need to make big changes because things are not working, then you likely need to make a paradigm change*." This is certainly what I needed. I spent years in a world of chaos and pain. I needed big changes and I needed them fast. A paradigm change sounds complicated but what it all boils down to is finding new ways of approaching old problems. This is easy if you can let go of all the ways you normally approach things. Easy to say and hard to do. This was the challenge that I faced in my own life and, for our company, it continues to be a challenge worth meeting.

In this book I hope you have discovered new ways of thinking and felt challenged by some of the ideas presented here. Perhaps you thought illness just happens, or some people are just lucky in what life offers them. In one way or another I think most people have some attachment to the idea that the external world has something to do with what is happening to them.

Understanding that we create our reality is a concept that has been around for a long time. Many, many people have talked and written about it – but what does it really mean and how far do you take that concept? It is easy to see how a person who is afraid to cross the street could, ultimately, in all their fear and confusion, create the accident they wanted to avoid. We call this a self-fulfilling prophecy. It is also widely understood today that "attitude" has a great influence on what happens to us. The whole power of positive thinking has resulted from this concept.

* See bibliography

But what if we create **everything** that happens to us? Could this possibly be true? When we think of natural disasters, we don't think about individual responsibility. Individuals don't create earthquakes – **or do they?** Could we collectively, as a species, be contributing to natural phenomena? Could the earth be reflecting the great distress that the human race is experiencing? And could the earth be mirroring this back to us, for the very purpose of getting our attention so that we can see how far off track we are? If this is so, it would be an exact replication of the process I observed in people over the last 20 years. Always, in every case, the external world was a mirror for the person's internal distress. The world provides endless opportunities to look at the constrictions within and for people to realign with their core essence.

Is there a link between the individual and the whole? You **bet** there is. We are part of everything and everything is part of us. So where does extraordinary live?

Everywhere, within everything and in everyone. The challenge is can we see the extraordinary within ourselves, wihin those we know and love and of equal importance, within all mankind? Imagine what our world would be like if this was to happen?

EXCELANATION™, EXCELABILITY™, AND EXCELESSENCE™.

EXCEL *ex·cel – to surpass in accomplishment or achievement*
ABILITY *abil·i·ty – natural aptitude or acquired proficiency*
ESSENCE *es·sence – all that makes a thing what it is; intrinsic value*

FOR OVER 20 YEARS I WAS DRIVEN BY AN UNSHAKABLE BELIEF that people can achieve profound and lasting change quickly. My dream was realized when I was able to refine my process into two streams, *Excelability* and *Excelessence*. The streams were created to optimize an individual's performance, well-being and health. *Excelessence* is for people seeking heightened well-being and optimum health. It identifies internal obstacles, limitations and fears, then releases internal constrictions, liberating our capacity to heal and discover the optimal joy in life.

Excelability is specifically designed for high achievers such as executives, CEOs, entrepreneurs and performing artists. It targets and releases internal obstacles, limitations and fears that prevent individuals from reaching their highest performance level. For optimal performance it's well recognized that the mind and body need to work in tandem. The mystery has always been how to attain and sustain this vital link. Performance in the flow, which

I describe as *effortless effort*, can deteriorate instantly when an internal constriction occurs; it operates in the same way a computer virus is triggered and ravages the system in moments. By addressing constrictions at the body's cellular level, the *Excelability* process releases the individual's capacity to perform at often undreamed-of levels.

The key to the remarkable success of both processes lies in the ability to clear constrictions at the body's cellular level. When change is made at this level, it is rapid, profound and long-lasting.

EXCELESSENCE – FOR WELL-BEING AND HEALTH

Many people define who they are by the experiences they have had, both painful and joyful; the jobs they do, their friends and family, their accomplishments, etc. Our true identity is linked to our **essence**, not our experiences. Excelessence is a process that re-establishes your awareness of your connection to your essence in a powerful and long-lasting way.

In this process you realign your system, and clear and release perceived interior obstacles, limitations and fears. This creates the freedom to be who you truly are, not who you were taught to think you *should* be. The balance that is created is so natural, it quickly becomes as familiar as the imbalance was. This natural state carries with it an attitude of reverence for all life and gratitude for what we have, rather than a focus on what is wrong. It connects us to the pulse of the universe and a sense of *Oneness* with every living thing.

Excelessence liberates the natural ability to achieve a full, vibrant and healthy life. It resolves internal conflicts and facilitates a transformation from dependence on external feedback to internal confidence and esteem. People move from uncertainty to knowing, from self-doubt to self-acceptance, from disease to health, and from lives that feel empty to clarity of purpose.

RESULTS IN THE FIELDS OF WELL-BEING AND HEALTH:

- Medical doctor overcomes eight years of Prozac use and Affective Seasonal Disorder in 10 days
- Government employee's "sick day" usage decreases by 93.75 per cent
- Severe stutterer freed from stuttering in two weeks
- Woman ends five years of disability from chronic fatigue and fibromyalgia in six weeks
- In one month a woman transforms seven chronic illnesses and is declared "healthy as a horse" by the medical profession
- Student with the worst documented case of ADHD on Prince Edward Island goes from 35 per cent average in remedial program to 80 per cent in regular program
- Nineteen-year-old university student with drinking problem reclaims healthy lifestyle
- Eight-year-old girl with severe rash, which had proven resistant to medical treatment for a month, enjoys clear skin in 48 hours
- Brain surgery patient's recovery declared "miracle" by medical profession
- Twenty-five years of suffering with Anorexia Nervosa is happily resolved as woman dissolves underlying cause

EXCELABILITY – FOR ENHANCED PERFORMANCE

Excelability increases performance and accesses unlimited potential in elite performers, athletes, artists, CEOs and entrepreneurs. The *Excelability* process, like *Excelessence*, clears internal obstacles, limitations and fears, freeing clients to realize their full potential.

This may be manifested in increased sales, level of confidence, and new ceilings for optimal performance. Athletes report continued increases in their personal bests. Their performance becomes a natural, balanced *effortless effort*. CEOs report working less and achieving more; having greater balance in their personal lives and enjoying closer relationships. Whether you are striving to achieve your best, to maintain it or to discover it, Excelability removes obstacles standing in the way.

213

EXAMPLES OF CORPORATE RESULTS:

- The best performance of a top international CEO accelerates from one day in seven to 75 per cent of the time
- Sales department increases top product output by 176 per cent and profits increase by 244 per cent in one year
- Fourteen sales representatives increase corporate productivity by 65.8 per cent over the previous year
- Executive home builder shifts production ceiling from eight homes per year to 15 in one year – an output increase of 87.5 per cent
- Sales associate catapults from lowest in sales to top departmental salesman in one year
- Entrepreneur goes from zero sales to closing two major contracts in two days

ENDORSEMENTS IN THE FIELD OF ATHLETICS:

- NHL player, in slump after experiencing injury-filled season, plays his best game of the season after 1.5 hours with Donn Smith. Two more hours saw him soar to the top of his game where he remained for the rest of the season.
- NHL player, told he would not be able to skate for 14 days after an ACL sprain, resumes League play on ninth day.
- University Men's Rowing Team assembled at last minute wins two gold and two silver medals at the Commonwealth Games and the gold medal at the World's University Rowing Competition.
- CFL field goal kicker's record climbs from 60 to 90 per cent field goal completions, and captures Grey Cup.
- National Hockey League team goes from .333 wins to .700 wins in last 11 games to clinch final playoff spot.
- After not winning all season, golfer wins five tournaments, tying three golf course records in span of one month.
- Arthritic pain due to sports injuries in hip, shoulder and knee vanishes

in 10 days, ending seven years of suffering.
- LPGA golfer increases earnings by 129 per cent in one season.
- Athlete secures position on World Championships, Pan American and Pan Pacific swim teams.

HOW ARE EXCELESSENCE AND EXCELABILITY UNIQUE?

Many approaches in the marketplace offer a way to alleviate emotional and psychological distress. They range from conventional talking therapy to encounter groups. Excelanation is different from other modalities in the way that it combines the following five factors.

- **Profound Depth:** The ability to locate the root of the one core constriction that gives rise to all the symptoms in the person's life. Historically, we have not had the tools to identify precisely this core or root cause that spawns all of a person's constricting beliefs. Now we have it. Working simultaneously with the triad of the intellect, the nervous system and the cellular structure, changes are deep and profound.

- **Revolutionary:** Erases constricting patterns at the cellular level through a sophisticated, respectful and effective process. This transmutes the energy that has been locked in a constricted form; this now expanded energy can flow through the system. The results are greater energy, expansiveness, vibrancy and activation of the body's natural healing and regenerative capacity.

- **Stunning Speed:** The shifts happen rapidly, often in the first session, and almost always within the first two sessions scheduled 10 days apart. This transformation is achieved through simultaneous shifts at a neurological level, which rewires the circuitry in the system. Once this occurs, change happens immediately and across all systems.

- **Systemic:** Impacts all systems (mental, emotional, spiritual, physical, neurological and cellular) simultaneously within the person in an integrated approach.

- **Immense Scope:** Cuts across traditional barriers of age, severity of symptoms and chronicity of issues in the areas of performance, health, energy and stress.

EXCELANATION: THE COMPANY

Fueled by the powerful knowledge that people can rapidly achieve profound and lasting personal transformation, the vision of Excelanation is to make available, globally, our Evolutionary Human Change Technology™. The rippling effects of this profound process are already being felt around the globe. Excelanation is dedicated to ongoing research and the delivery of our leading-edge processes in order to achieve balance in a healthier, happier world of human interconnectedness.

For any further information please contact us at www.excelanation.com

BIBLIOGRAPHY

Peter R. Breggin, M.D., *Talking Back to Prozac*, St. Martin's Press, New York, NY, 1994.

Peter R. Breggin, M.D., *Talking Back to Ritalin*, Common Courage Press, Monroe, ME, 1998.

Peter R. Breggin, M.D., *Your Drug May Be Your Problem*, Perseus Books, Redding, MA, 1999.

Deepak Chopra M.D., *Ageless Body, Timeless Mind*, Random House, New York, NY, 1993.

Glenn Clark, *The Man Who Tapped the Secrets of the Universe*, University of Science & Philosophy, Waynesboro, VA, 1989.

Steven Covey, *Principle Centered Leadership*, Simon & Schuster, New York, NY, 1992.

Robert Dilts, *Changing Belief Systems with Neuro Linguistic Programming*, Meta Publications, Capitola, CA.

Robert Dilts, Tim Hallbam and Suzi Smith, *Beliefs: Pathways to Health and Well-being*, Metamorphous Press, Portland, OR.

Michael J. Fox, *Lucky Man*, Hyperion Press, New York, NY, 2002.

William Glasser, M.D., *Positive Addictions*, HarperCollins, New York, NY, 1976.

The Guardian, Charlottetown, PEI, 1996.

David R. Hawkins M.D., Ph. D., *Power versus Force*, Hay House, Carlsbad, CA, 2002.

Harville Hendricks, Ph.D., *Getting the Love You Want*, Henry Holt, New York, NY, 1992.

The International Center for the Study of Psychiatry and Psychology (ICSPP), Newsletter, Summer 2002.

Gabor Mate M.D., *Scattered Minds – A New Look at the Origins and Healing of Attention Deficit*, Knopf Canada, Toronto, ON, 1999.

Caroline Myss, *Anatomy of the Spirit*, Harmony Books, New York, NY, 1996.

Caroline Myss, *Energy Anatomy*, Audio Cassette, Sounds True, Louisville, CO, 1997.

Norman Vincent Peale, *The Power of Positive Thinking*, Simon & Schuster, New York, NY, 1997, 3rd Edition.

Norman Vincent Peale, *Positive Thinking for a Time Like This*, Prentice Hall, Upper Saddle River, NJ, 1975.

James Redfield, *Celestine Prophecy*, Warner Books, New York, NY, 1994.

James Redfield, *The Tenth Insight*, Warner Books, New York, NY, 1996.

James Redfield, *The Secret of Shambala*, Warner Books, New York, NY, 1999.

Anthony Robbins, *Unlimited Power*, Simon & Schuster, New York, NY, 1986.

Debbie Shapiro, *The Bodymind Workbook*, Elements Books, 1990.

Bernie S. Siegal, M.D., *Love, Medicine & Miracles*, HarperCollins, New York, NY, 1986.

Eckhart Tolle, *The Power of Now*, New World Library, Novato, CA, 1999.

John E. Veltheim, D.C., *The BodyTalk System*, Paperback, Lightening Source, La Vergne, TN, 1999.

Gary Zukav, *Seat of the Soul*, Fireside, Raleigh, NC, 1990.

Donn is a man with a great heart and immense compassion. His dream is to make a difference in the world, to ease people's suffering. But dreams are rarely simple to realize. It took him 23 years, with courage and tenacity, to develop and refine a model that would assist people in making powerful and profound changes.

Donn currently lives in scenic West Vancouver with his partner Rosy. Much of his creativity flows out of his meditations at the ocean's edge in the early hours of the morning. This practice of meditation has been a cornerstone for Donn's insights and facilitates his connection to the universal energy that surrounds us all.

To relax, Donn plays golf, skis, rides a Harley-Davidson motorcycle, dances and captains a speedboat. However, he enjoys work as much as he does play. Donn's diverse training background and his natural talent, combined with his ability to apply his expertise to any performance arena, produces amazing results. He has worked with a wide range of organizations, companies and associations including entrepreneurs, executives, business teams, government agencies, sports teams, elite athletes, coaches and scouts.

The key to Donn's heart is family; his big smile shines when asked about someone near and dear to him. He enjoys regular visits from his children and grandchildren. His son Trevor visits from Japan, and his daughter Shelly travels to Vancouver from Prince Edward Island with her husband Gordon, son Daniel, and daughter Makenzie. Although these people are "family," what is unique about Donn is how quickly you feel like family in his presence.

219

Lynn's family experience formed the foundation for her values of caring and compassion. Her parents' inter-racial marriage, unusual for that era, modeled for her the power of love. Adopting five children was another example of her parents' courage and set the stage for Lynn's willingness to 'take a different path.'

Lynn has a Master's degree in Social Work from the University of Toronto and over twenty years' experience in private practice. She has a wide range of skills in counseling, training and consulting and has worked extensively with individuals, systems and organizations. She connects quickly with people and brings clarity to the challenges presented. Lynn's unique combination of energy, compassion and focus makes her an impressive trainer and she's often invited to teach in Australia, New Zealand, Ireland and North and South America.

Lynn's role at Excelanation is threefold: she works directly with clients, is Co-Director of Training, and a member of the Visioning Team, which contributes to the creative development of Excelanation. Her exceptional ability to express herself verbally and her keen attention to detail were among the personal qualities that prepared her to co-author this book.

For Lynn, writing this book has been an opportunity to express many deeply held values and beliefs. One of her greatest rewards has been expressing these beliefs in her relationship with her son Timothy. This open and loving relationship embodies her commitment to building a better world for future generations.

 Steve's life purpose is to leave the world a better place for others by learning ways to improve quality of life and then sharing what he has learned. This mission overlapped seamlessly with Donn Smith's dream, and he brings skill and wit to all projects, including his contributions to the writing of this book.

After receiving his doctorate in psychology from Northwestern University in Evanston, Illinois in 1975, Steve became a professor of psychology at the University of Winnipeg, Manitoba until 1990. He began his counseling practice in 1980, working with individuals, couples and families as they faced health concerns, parenting challenges, relationship difficulties, stress management, issues of low self esteem, depression, anxiety, trauma, and performance enhancement.

In 1990 he became an international trainer in a variety of topics including Neuro-Linguistic Programming, a model for enhancing performance, updating limiting beliefs, and improving communications. These skills have proven invaluable for government groups, corporations, training groups and individuals in Hong Kong, Taiwan, New Zealand, Australia, the United States, and across Canada.

Steve lives with his wife, Dawn, on the mountainside in West Vancouver, giving thanks daily for their astounding view of the Vancouver area and beyond. For recreation he loves hiking in the mountains, travel and times with friends and family. His two daughters, Tanya and Tori, live in Victoria, BC. Tori's sons, Dylan and Theron, add their youthful zest to his life whenever they visit.